School Finance Elections

A Comprehensive Planning Model for Success

Second Edition

Don E. Lifto
J. Bradford Senden

Published in partnership with the
American Association of School Administrators

ROWMAN & LITTLEFIELD EDUCATION
A division of
Rowman & Littlfield Publishers, Inc.
Lanham • New York • Toronto • Plymouth, UK

Published in partnership with the American Association of School Administrators

Published by Rowman & Littlefield Education
A division of Rowman & Littlefield Publishers, Inc.
A wholly owned subsidiary of The Rowman & Littlefield Publishing Group, Inc.
4501 Forbes Boulevard, Suite 200, Lanham, Maryland 20706
http://www.rowmaneducation.com

Estover Road, Plymouth PL6 7PY, United Kingdom

British Library Cataloguing in Publication Information Available

Library of Congress Cataloging-in-Publication Data

Lifto, Don E., 1949-
  School finance elections : a comprehensive planning model for success / Don
E. Lifto J. Bradford Senden. — 2nd ed.
    p. cm.
  "Published in partnership with the American Association of School Adminis-
trators."
  ISBN 978-1-60709-148-6 (hardcover : alk. paper) — ISBN 978-1-60709-149-
3 (pbk. : alk. paper) — ISBN 978-1-60709-150-9 (ebook)
  1. Education—United States—Finance. 2. School elections—United States-
-Planning. 3. School taxes—United States. I. Senden, J. Bradford, 1949- II.
American Association of School Administrators. III. Title. LB2825.L485
2010
    371.2'06—dc22   2009033212

⊗ ™ The paper used in this publication meets the minimum requirements of
American National Standard for Information Sciences—Permanence of Paper
for Printed Library Materials, ANSI/NISO Z39.48-1992.
Printed in the United States of America

Contents

Foreword

Executing a successful school finance election can be one of the most important—yet also one of the most difficult—responsibilities a school system leader faces. School leaders have to be not only adept at planning for school needs but also political salespersons who can sell the public on a school's needs and convince them they need to put aside their private needs for the public good. Whether a school finance election involves a vote on a tax levy or a school bond measure, effective leadership is essential to winning on election day.

In the pages that follow, Don Lifto and Brad Senden provide a recipe for success at the ballot box. They offer practical, research-based advice for preparing an election campaign, anticipating potential challenges, and managing the process for a successful outcome.

They divide their comprehensive planning model into the key elements of school finance elections. These include using a research-based approach, targeting messages strategically using voter files and demographic maps, analyzing and learning lessons from past elections, seeking community feedback through surveys, crafting effective ballot questions, using effective communications to target and engage the public, writing a detailed campaign plan, identifying effective campaign leaders, and carrying out the plan.

In addition to these core lessons, this fully revised and updated second edition of *School Finance Elections* provides new information about applications for the Internet in school finance election campaigns. It also includes new research on organized opposition, which the authors call "the foe of special elections requiring taxpayer approval." Lifto and Senden warn that those who oppose a campaign, even if small in number, can be highly organized and have considerable reach and impact, especially when aided by the latest electronic communication tools.

Today, school finance elections are often won and lost by small margins. With such little room for error, anyone involved in planning and conducting a school finance election should read this book carefully.

Daniel A. Domenech
Executive Director
American Association of School Administrators
Arlington, Virginia

Acknowledgments

For the two of us, rewriting and expanding this book has again been a labor of love and an opportunity to put to paper what we have learned about school finance elections over more than two decades. Some of the learning has been research based and theoretical in nature, and for that knowledge we thank our teachers—the professors, researchers, political pundits, and various experts who have shared their wisdom over the years. Much of the learning was—and continues to be—on-the-job training, honing our skills in the trenches of hundreds of school finance elections, working hand in hand with superintendents, school board members, principals, parent leaders, and countless campaign volunteers. Although the thrill of victory is certainly more fun, we often learn more in the tears of unfulfilled expectations. For these experiences and the opportunity to work with hundreds of talented people we are grateful. For all who took the time to read and comment on the first edition of this book, we are thankful and greatly appreciate your comments and ideas.

We also want to again thank and acknowledge our able editor, Carrie Ardito, for her assistance.

Lastly, and most importantly, we thank our families for their love and support throughout our careers, and in particular for their continuing encouragement to improve and expand what we hope remains an important book for school administrators and school districts as they strive to meet the facility and financial needs of public school students at the ballot box.

In particular, we want to thank Jessica Senden for technical advice about the use of social networks.

Don E. Lifto, Ph.D.
J. Bradford Senden, Ph.D.

Introduction

"Education officials need to furnish leadership in school elections . . . an unsuccessful election reduces educational opportunities for students" (Kimbrough and Nunnery, 1971, p. 4). Who can argue with this simple statement? Providing effective leadership, however, is not that easy. Research and practice have yet to yield an election formula that always produces winners. Whether it is a request for bricks and mortar or more operating money, each election type and context are unique, with no guarantee that a set of campaign strategies that are wildly successful in one district will not fail in your community. If successful campaigns were *not* such a delicate balance of science and art, the key to success would have long since been discovered, resulting in significantly more school districts winning at the ballot box.

Alumni parents provide us with a wonderful example of the evolving nature of school tax elections and the complex components involved in their success. Our research on the "tight fisted" character of alumni parents—within the context of the demographics of baby boomers, global economic malaise, and the increase in technology-savvy opposition groups—does not bode well for school tax elections. Many states report lower passage rates for school tax issues in recent years in comparison to what had been the norm over time. This "perfect storm" of demographic, economic, political, and technological drivers will make it considerably more difficult to meet the operational and facility needs of public school students going forward. This challenging reality makes it all the more important that school leaders understand and have the ability to effectively use research and best practices when it is necessary to seek approval at the ballot box.

This book represents a marriage of research and successful practice, presenting a comprehensive planning model for school leaders who are preparing for and conducting school tax elections. The emphasis is on systems and strategies rather than specific campaign tactics. Avoiding a myopic focus on tactics allows school leaders to elevate their thinking to a more comprehensive and long-range vision of election planning. Each of the chapters elaborates on one or more of the 10 elements in our comprehensive planning model (see figure I.1). Use of this model has reaped

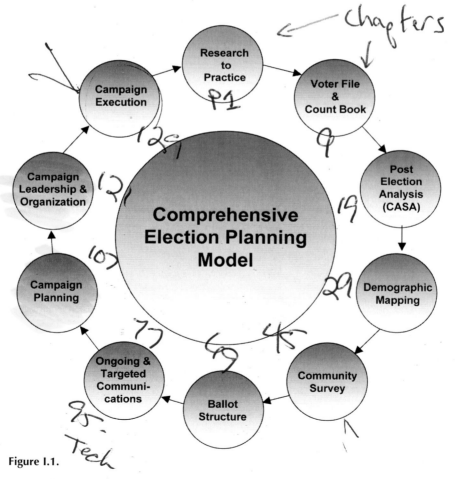

Figure I.1.

success in all types of school districts from New Jersey to California, and we hope that it brings you success at the ballot box as well.

ELEMENT 1: RESEARCH TO PRACTICE

Although there is no pat formula for success, school leaders should not be discouraged from rolling up their sleeves, digging in, and becoming students of sound research and successful practices. In the final analysis, there is no better road map to a successful election. In fact, university libraries are replete with dissertations documenting that winning campaigns use research-based strategies to a *greater extent* and *more effectively* than unsuccessful elections. Understanding the research on school tax elections and thoughtfully implementing these strategies are the foundations of winning campaigns.

ELEMENT 2: VOTER FILE AND COUNT BOOK

The voter file and count book represent the district's master election dossier, which details essential information about your campaign's key resources—the voters. By integrating files of registered voters, parents, preschool families, and past supporters, the district's campaign is provided with a powerful tool for planning, canvassing, targeting messages, and implementing get-out-the-vote strategies.

ELEMENT 3: POST-ELECTION ANALYSIS

It is important to keep one eye on the rearview mirror as you drive toward your next election. A thorough understanding and analysis of your district's prior elections are a prerequisite to effectively executing your next campaign. By integrating data from voting records with the parent file, school leaders can gain a more precise understanding of past voter participation and therefore can better predict future voter behavior. We have coined the acronym CASA to describe this process, which stands for Collect, Analyze, Summarize, and Archive.

ELEMENT 4: DEMOGRAPHIC MAPPING

Demographic mapping merges current census data, which contains a multitude of information about the district, with registered voter and parent data found in the annotated voter file. This information is displayed in color maps and provides school and volunteer leaders with a better understanding of the school district and strategic information from which to plan and execute the campaign.

ELEMENT 5: COMMUNITY SURVEY

Aligning the community's values and appetite for spending with what the school district actually needs and puts on the ballot is paramount to success. A random sample of registered voters is drawn from the annotated voter file, which mirrors the demography of the school district. The community survey, typically based on a 12- to 14-minute telephone interview administered four to eight months prior to the election date, provides the school district with vital information about what the community thinks and is likely to support. Conducting a survey closer to the election decreases exposure to those political, economic, or social events that may change the landscape in the time between collecting data and casting votes. The disadvantage of surveying close to election day is narrowing the window of time available to educate and change voter opinion. Many school districts maximize the advantages of both approaches by doing a baseline survey a year or more before a planned tax election, getting the "lay of the land" in terms of voters' perspectives, implementing community engagement strategies to educate and persuade, and then following with a short tracking survey just before the school board needs to make a final decision on the structure and content of the ballot.

ELEMENT 6: BALLOT QUESTIONS

When the voters enter the voting booth, what will they see? In most states, ballots can contain a single proposal or multiple questions. Will each of the ballot questions be freestanding (i.e., winning or losing on their own merits) or will passage of the second or third question be contingent on the first proposal getting a thumbs up? The decision about the content and structure of the ballot is critical and must be guided by the district's election history and the community survey results.

ELEMENT 7: ONGOING AND TARGETED COMMUNICATIONS

Developing a compelling message and directing it to parents just prior to an election used to be good enough, but not anymore. In today's election environment, providing high-quality, ongoing communication throughout the year is essential. The election campaign builds on this foundation by developing core and subordinate messages and targeting them to unique audiences. The annotated voter file and cross-tabulated results found in the community survey provide the data from which to plan an effective communication strategy.

ELEMENT 8: TASKS AND TIMELINES

Planning and executing a school tax election is, for most school administrators, one of the most complex and challenging leadership tasks they will encounter. A common reason for failure is lack of coordination between what the school district is doing and the activities of volunteers working in support of the election. Remember, if there isn't a written plan, it does not exist. Key campaign activities must be spelled out, coordinated, and scheduled on a day-to-day and week-to-week basis to ensure that no one drops the ball.

ELEMENT 9: CAMPAIGN LEADERSHIP

Merely *understanding* the need to involve a community in a grassroots effort falls well short of the target when it comes to successful tax elections. Your campaign can be well on its way toward a victory if you are strategic and focused on recruiting the "ideal task performer" for each and every leadership need. Do not send your campaign volunteers out into the community until they are thoroughly prepared and trained. And last, plan carefully for the appropriate role for the school board, administrators, staff, and community.

ELEMENT 10: CAMPAIGN EXECUTION

Pick your analogy—sports, ballet, business, or politics—they are one in the same. All of the research, planning, and training in the world will not matter if the school district, in cooperation with the campaign committee, cannot effectively execute the plan. The efforts of the school district and campaign committee must be driven by passion and an unrelenting commitment to success that is girded by high-quality execution from beginning to end.

Now it's time to dive into the details. Each chapter builds on the last as we provide school district leaders with sound advice about the planning and execution of school tax elections.

1

Research to Practice

You thought you did everything right. You devoured the research, interrogated winning superintendents from Albuquerque to Azusa, and replicated successful campaign strategies from neighboring school districts. But when the ballots were finally counted, you found yourself on the losing end of an important school tax election. What happened?

Since there is no pat formula for success, school leaders should roll up their sleeves, dig in, and become students of sound research and successful practice. In the final analysis, there is no better road map to a successful election. In fact, university libraries are replete with dissertations documenting that winning campaigns use research-based strategies to a *greater extent* and *more effectively* than unsuccessful ones. Understanding the research on school tax elections and thoughtfully implementing these strategies form the foundation of a successful campaign.

To begin with, it is important to avoid a potentially shortsighted focus on campaign tactics and achieve a more comprehensive understanding of the research related to school tax elections. Without a basic understanding of the research-based variables most often associated with success, school leaders can easily slip into a frantic strategy of piecing together a hodgepodge of tactics from the archives of successful elections. Distributing the Top 10 reasons to vote "yes" inside fortune cookies might have been a hit in a neighboring district, but this tactic could bomb in your community unless done within the context of a comprehensive, research-based election plan. School leaders need to understand that broad campaign strategies and the specific tactics to achieve them must be built on and flow from a foundation of election research.

The research of Philip Piele and John Hall, completed 35 years ago, still provides the foundation for many contemporary dissertations and scholarly works on this topic. *Budgets, Bonds, and Ballots* (1973) summarizes more than a decade of research by analyzing and categorizing 61 election variables. Research studies for each of the variables are labeled as being significantly positive, negative, or at least statistically related to the results of these elections. Their research summary emphasizes the difference between contextual variables (e.g., wealth) that are generally out of the practitioner's control and specific campaign strategies selected by a school leader. Understanding and applying election research within the unique context of a school community is part of the art of leadership within this framework. The campaign plan then becomes a carefully woven fabric of strategies designed to interact with and influence the environment within the school district. Dozens of other authors build on Piele and Hall's "megastudy," carrying the research forward into the present day. In the course of writing this book, we revisited the body of research conducted in the 1980s and 1990s but also analyzed more than 30 additional studies completed through 2009.

What have we learned about school elections over the last 35 years? In our experience, the following 11 factors are most often associated, in both research and practice, with successful school tax elections. In combination, they form the foundation for our planning model.

FACTOR 1: UNANIMOUS ELECTION RESOLUTION AND SUPPORT BY THE SCHOOL BOARD THROUGHOUT THE CAMPAIGN

School board solidarity is one of 20 variables examined by Piele and Hall (1973), with all studies pointing to a positive correlation between unanimity and successful elections. T. N. Pullium (1983) asserts that "total support by members of the school board is almost always necessary for the success of a school referendum" (p. 50). Another researcher more bluntly warns, "A school board whose members have not reached a consensus on the content and format of the referendum should not embark on a campaign" (Etheredge,

1989, p. 46). Blount (1991), Dunbar (1991), Brummer (1999), and Mobley (2007) cite similar findings. Clearly, this is a critical factor demanding attention long before a proposal is placed on the school board agenda.

FACTOR 2: COMMUNITY HAS HIGH LEVELS OF TRUST, SATISFACTION, AND PERCEPTIONS OF QUALITY FOR ITS PUBLIC SCHOOLS

School districts would be well advised to borrow from the Ford Motor Company tagline and "make quality Job 1." Lifto and Morris (2000) focus on the quality question in their evaluation of 107 Minnesota school tax elections between 1996 and 2000. The common variable in each of the campaigns was pre-election polling during which they asked, "How would you rate the quality of education in your public schools—excellent, good, only fair, or poor?"

How important is quality in relationship to school tax elections? In this study, 96 percent of the cases revealed that the size of the negative evaluation (i.e., fair or poor) discriminated between winning and losing campaigns. When more than 17 percent of the public gave their public schools fair or poor marks, 27 out of 30 elections failed. By comparison, when less than 17 percent rated their schools fair or poor, 76 out of 77 elections passed.[1] Maintaining a core value of quality as Job 1 is essential because "success at the polls is substantially driven by how your community views the quality of its public schools" (Lifto and Morris, 2000, p. 17). Studies by Corrick (1995), Phillips (1995), Williamson (1997), Schrom (2004), and Faltys (2006) echo the importance of residents' perceptions of quality and continuous improvement.

FACTOR 3: COMPREHENSIVE CAMPAIGN PLANNING AND EFFECTIVE EXECUTION BASED ON CURRENT RESEARCH, BEST PRACTICES, AND DEMOGRAPHIC CHARACTERISTICS OF THE COMMUNITY

The ability to understand and effectively apply election research in a particular context is critical and positively correlates with success. More than three decades of research emphasize the importance of comprehensive planning and use of research-based strategies. Piele and Hall (1973), acting as pragmatists, remind school leaders that using research, conducting comprehensive planning, and then executing a world-class campaign are all within the control of the practitioner and *do* matter. J. F. Henderson Jr.'s study of Colorado school elections matches election outcomes with use of nine key campaign strategies. The more these factors were used, the more likely the election was successful (Henderson, 1986). Underscoring that a cookie-cutter approach does not work, Williamson (1997) concludes that school districts are more successful when research and campaign strategies are adapted to the community's values and demographic characteristics.

FACTOR 4: OUTSTANDING PUBLIC RELATIONS THROUGHOUT THE YEAR, TAILORED TO UNIQUE AUDIENCES WITHIN THE DISTRICT AND FOCUSED ON THE PURPOSE, BENEFITS, AND CONSEQUENCES OF A SUCCESSFUL OR UNSUCCESSFUL ELECTION

Serving as a foundation for successful tax elections, the quality of public engagement and related communication strategies are evident throughout the research. The most successful districts achieve three key attributes when it comes to public relations:

- Outstanding quality.
- Ongoing public relations.
- Focused messages to different audiences emphasizing the proposal's purpose and benefits.

One researcher highlighted the need for ongoing engagement by warning campaigners not to "commit the fatal error [of] trying to educate the electorate while at the same time urging school supporters to vote" (Etheredge, 1989, p. 34). As the percentage of registered voters with children who are public school students continues to decrease, it is also important to develop the capacity to communicate multiple messages to a number of audiences. A multitude of researchers, including Lode (1999), Hinson

(2001), Neill (2003), and Clemens (2003), would join the choir in emphasizing similar conclusions.

FACTOR 5: SCIENTIFIC POLLING IS USED TO BETTER UNDERSTAND THE COMMUNITY'S PERCEPTIONS, UNDERSTANDING, AND READINESS FOR PROPOSAL

Designing and administering a scientific poll drawn from the school district's registered voter file is one of the most important pre-election activities and positively correlates with success. In addition to studying the community's understanding and support for the district's proposal, surveys also provide the opportunity to benchmark key community perceptions (e.g., overall quality or financial management), some of which are linked with success and all of which will help target effective communications to key audiences. Basing decisions on reliable survey data is a potent political strategy closely tied to winning elections and integral to effective campaign communication. Dalton (1995) and Henderson (1997) each authored contemporary studies linking scientific surveys to success.

FACTOR 6: PROPOSAL REFLECTS STRONG ALIGNMENT BETWEEN ITS PURPOSE AND COST AND THE COMMUNITY'S PRIORITIES AND WILLINGNESS TO PAY HIGHER TAXES

School leaders must determine how to align the ballot question with what the community wants because "each district has its own collective demand for education under varying tax cost conditions" (Sclafani, 1985, p. 25). When it comes to school tax elections, alignment has two dimensions: the "what" or content of the proposal and the "how much" or the cost and tax impact. A campaign supporting the district has an advantage when the ballot question is congruent on both counts, aligning with the values of the community *and* its collective willingness to pay in the form of higher property taxes. Dalton (1995), Galton (1996), Brummer (1999), Hinson (2001), Friedland (2002), and Clemens (2003) document similar results.

FACTOR 7: BROAD-BASED AND STRATEGIC COMMUNITY INVOLVEMENT IN PLANNING AND EXECUTING A CAMPAIGN

Although "flying under the radar" may be an appealing approach in some communities, the preponderance of evidence suggests that broad, strategic community involvement is paramount to success in most circumstances. Few communities enjoy the luxury of having public school children in more than one-third of their households. As a result, if a district expects to garner sufficient support to win the election, significant community involvement is usually the only option. It is important to note that community involvement has important quantitative *and* qualitative dimensions. Elections are more successful when the ideal task performers are recruited for specific campaign functions. Henderson (1997), Brummer (1999), Lode (1999), Friedland (2002), Pappalardo (2005), and Geurink (2008) are just a few of the many researchers who have positively correlated broad community involvement with successful elections.

FACTOR 8: EFFECTIVE USE OF VOTER FILE AND OTHER INTEGRATED DATABASES TO TARGET, CANVASS, AND DELIVER "YES" VOTERS TO THE POLLS

One of the challenges facing school leaders during a school tax election is to "remember that a referendum is a political—not an education—campaign" (Etheredge, 1989, p. 39). Grassroots committees seeking to elect candidates to local, state, and national office have long relied on registered voter files as the backbone of effective campaign work. It is the voter history files, parent files, and past-supporter archives that provide key data for voter targeting, focused communications, and get-out-the-vote efforts. Drawing the random sample for the survey from the voter history file allows the campaign to link key survey findings with particular blocs of citizens in the voter file and their likelihood of voting in the school tax election. Quantitative and qualitative studies by researchers such as True (1996), Williamson (1997), Lode (1999), Kinsall (2000), and Pappalardo (2005) support the use of data to target, canvass, and effectively get the "yes" voters to the polls.

FACTOR 9: SUCCESS IN OBTAINING KEY VIP AND ORGANIZATIONAL ENDORSEMENTS

Dravis Brod (handwritten)

"The personal influence of influentials (opinion leaders) may be a critical factor in legitimizing (making acceptable) school proposals among voters" (Kimbrough and Nunnery, 1971, pp. 50–54). Identifying and engaging the power structure within a community can be a significant factor in determining an election's outcome. Doing so can be easier in smaller, more stable communities compared with sprawling suburbs where influence is more diffused. Endorsements from the media and key organizations can also be very helpful in building a base of community support. Developing relationships with these individuals and groups should be an important ongoing component of community engagement strategies. True (1996) and Stockton (1996) cite the positive influence of endorsements.

FACTOR 10: ABSENCE OF COMMUNITY CONFLICT AND AVOIDANCE OF ORGANIZED OPPOSITION

Significant community conflict and the organized opposition it often yields are difficult to overcome even with the best of campaigns. The distraction of conflict is bad enough, but even worse is that "citizens stimulated to vote by this community conflict have a tendency to cast negative ballots" (Chandler, 1989, pp. 21–22). Although it is impossible to completely control this variable, school leaders can use two strategies to minimize the damage. First, while "it may be impossible to eliminate tax resistance, . . . it can be controlled by attempting to reduce other controversies" (Allen, 1985, p. 94). For example, if your district needs to redo elementary boundaries, perhaps it can wait until after the election. School leaders should also attempt to "negotiate positions between influentials . . . so that the needs of education and children are not held hostage by two warring factions" (Kimbrough and Nunnery, 1971, pp. 22–23). Galton (1996), Day (1996), Franklin (1997), Friedland (2002), and Mobley (2007) authored other studies documenting the effect of conflict and organized opposition.

FACTOR 11: SUCCESSFUL TAX ELECTIONS OFTEN INCLUDE FUNDING FOR TECHNOLOGY AND INFORMATION ABOUT SITE-SPECIFIC IMPROVEMENTS

For the community that may be more self-centered and less egalitarian than in the past, communicating site-specific improvements is increasingly important. Many voters will be influenced by how the proposed improvements will affect *their* children or *their* neighborhood school. The almost universal desire for a school district to remain technologically advanced can also be a key factor. In a study of Oklahoma bond campaigns, Beckham (2001) found that elections were six times more likely to pass if they included an investment in technology. The higher the investment, the more likely the election would pass. Other researchers, including Williamson (1997) and Hockersmith (2001), drew parallel conclusions.

Research matters, regardless of whether it is quantitative studies and chi-square tests or qualitative studies and triangulation. Hundreds of studies have been done since the publication of *Budgets, Bonds, and Ballots* (1973) against a backdrop of tens of thousands of school tax elections. This adds up to a substantial body of research and successful practice from which to draw. It is incumbent upon school leaders to build their election planning on this foundation and develop research-based strategies appropriate for their unique contexts. By doing so, more school districts will be successful on election day and more students will have their educational needs met in our nation's public schools.

NOTE

1. The null hypothesis—that quality had nothing to do with elections success or failure—was rejected at the 0.005 level.

2

The Voter File and Count Book

Like Biff in *Back to the Future II*, we have all had the fantasy that we can see the future and make a killing by either buying the right lottery ticket or betting on the right team. However, it is impossible to develop a clear view of the future by traveling through time. Fortunately, school finance campaigns have access to resources that do offer a clear picture of the future. The first of these tools—one that dramatically increases the value of all other campaign tools—is a fully annotated voter file.

Strategically, an annotated voter file allows campaign organizers to predict who will vote in any upcoming election by looking at who participated in the majority of the community's recent elections. This knowledge enables a campaign to focus its volunteer hours and campaign dollars where they will have the greatest impact. Rather than starting with a list of everyone with a telephone number or all of the parents in the district, a campaign can explode out of the starting gate with a list of those residents most likely to vote in a community election. Furthermore, instead of assuming that all parents will vote in the election, the campaign can, for example, develop a list of those parents who have trouble getting to the polls. The purpose of a voter file is to maintain focus not only on the voters who will always vote but also on the campaign's supporters who might forget to cast a ballot. A voter file makes all campaign-related efforts more efficient and more effective.

Now for the details. A voter file is a list of all of the school district's registered voters. In this electronic age, the information is available in various formats from a variety of sources. The county elections office or the office of the secretary of state in the state capitol should be your first stop.[1] When a source for voter information at the county or state level has been identified, the campaign should request instructions for ordering voter data—preferably in an electronic format to avoid the daunting task of manually entering voter records.

Where Do I Find Voter Files?

One Web site that can be very useful in looking for voter files from government sources is www.statelocalgov.net/index.cfn. From this site, one can easily find the secretary of state's Web site for each of the 50 states. For private voter file vendors, try www.vcsnet.com, www .catalist.us, or www.aristotle.com. Each will take you to a major list vendor's site.

Voter files can also be purchased from commercial vendors. These companies often offer two benefits above and beyond data you can obtain from a governmental source. First, private vendors generally provide their data in user-friendly formats and often over the Internet. For example, a vendor's software package may allow the user to easily produce the lists and labels needed for an effective campaign. Other vendors provide lists to which additional data enhancements (e.g., phone numbers) have been added. Second, most vendors provide data that are in a uniform structure in which voter history information is already integrated. However, prior to purchasing voter data from a commercial vendor, you should inquire about any restrictions the vendor has placed on the data. For example, a vendor may sell you data for use in *one* mailing or *one* set of phone canvass lists and you will be charged if you use the data a second time.

Determining the source of your campaign's voter data will depend largely on the computer expertise of your volunteers. Specifically, your campaign will need the expertise of a database programmer if you acquire data in an unfamiliar format. In many cases, voter data arrives in a tab-delimited ASCII file and, in many places, the vote history is stored in a separate ASCII file. Although you will not need someone capable of supporting the data needs of a Fortune 500 company, you will need someone comfortable with the manipulation of data in programs such as Excel, FoxPro, FileMaker, or Access.

What Do I Do with a Voter File?

- Count the number of voters in the community to more effectively plan your campaign.
- Produce lists and labels for mail and phone contact with very specific, targeted audiences.
- Store the results of all voter contact completed by the campaign.

Conversely, if your campaign acquires data in a ready-to-use software package, you will not need someone with data manipulation experience. However, you need to consider other limitations. Campaign software is designed to complete prespecified tasks based on the campaign experience and understanding of the private data vendor. Far too often, campaigns believe software can do anything. Nothing could be further from the truth. Your software must be designed to support the type of campaign you plan to run. Like every strategy in your campaign toolbox, you must have the right tool for *your* campaign.

Once you have identified a source for voter information, you need to know what you are looking for and the kind of information you can expect to find. The core of a voter file is the full legal name and residential address of each voter in the district. In addition, voter files generally contain a record of each individual's voting activity,[2] the voting district or precinct assigned to the individual's address,[3] a telephone number, the date on which the person registered to vote, and the individual's date of birth. There also may be information about his or her party affiliation, race, birthplace, and/or mailing address.

When requesting an electronic copy of your district's voter records, always request a *file layout*. A file layout provides the names of the data fields contained in the voter file. For example, some voter files store the voter's name in three data fields: first name, middle name, and last name. Others provide you with one data field that separates the last name of the voter from the first and middle names with a comma. The file layout will tell you not only how the data are stored in the voter file but also the number of characters you can expect to find in each data field. Without file layout information, you may not be able to successfully figure out where one data field begins and another ends. More important, you may not be able to tell what you have and therefore may discard valuable voter information.

Each piece of information in the voter file can be very useful in planning a school finance campaign. Some of the most important pieces of information are:

- *Residential address.* This information has obvious value if you want to write or visit a voter. It is also important because the address can be used to link the voter file to an electronic list of all parents in the district or an assessor's file. The residential address is also essential to append U.S. Census information into the voter file.
- *Mailing address.* In most cases, a voter's mailing address is the same as his or her residential address. There are, however, voters who have requested that any information from the registrar be mailed to an alternate address. There are also communities where the post office will only deliver to P.O. Box addresses. In these communities, you will need to use the mailing address given for each voter if you want your campaign mail to get delivered. The street addresses you will find in the records for this type of community are part of the 911 emergency services system but are not used by the postal service.
- *Voting activity.* The amount of information about an individual's level of voting activity varies from state to state and from private vendor to private vendor. In some states (e.g., Minnesota, Indiana, and Kentucky), complete multiyear voter histories come with the voter file. In others (e.g., California), you will be asked to specify the election information you want. Whatever the case, you want as much voter history as you can obtain because a voter's individual record of voting activity provides a wealth of information about who will show up for your election.
- *Voting district or precinct.* Every address in a voter file is assigned to a voting district or precinct. This information is important for two reasons. First, you will want to generate lists sorted by precinct to facilitate the coordination of volunteer activities in specific neighborhoods. Very often, school finance campaigns assign each precinct

to one of the district's elementary attendance areas. This process of assignment allows the campaign to give volunteers from each school lists of voters in the neighborhoods closest to the school. Second, just prior to the election you can link a voter's precinct name to the polling place assigned to that precinct. Linking this information enables the campaign to tell voters where they will vote. Furthermore, knowing the precinct is essential if you are campaigning in a state that allows poll watching and you intend to monitor polls on election day to see if your supporters are voting.

- *Registration date.* Knowing when a voter registered provides a campaign with two valuable pieces of information. First, the registration date can be used as a proxy for the length of time a person has lived in the district. For example, if long-term community residents need a great deal of information about the school finance election, registration date information can help target them for supplemental communications. Second, the registration date can be used in conjunction with an individual's voting history to identify "future frequent voters."

- *Birth date.* An individual's birth date enables you to calculate an individual's age. If you find there are voters for whom there is no record of a birth date, do not panic. Simply find out if your elections office has always been required to ask for a birth date when individuals register to vote. If, for example, they have only been collecting birth dates for the last 15 or 20 years, your file will contain a number of "no agers" who are actually relatively long-term district residents. If there are no birth dates in the voter file, it is safe to assume that your state or county is probably still not collecting them.

- *Party affiliation.* Party-related data may come in a number of forms or may not be available at all. Some states (e.g., California and Kentucky) ask individuals to declare a party when they register. This generally means that everyone in the file will have either a party affiliation or a record of his or her declaration to decline party selection. You may also find members of rather obscure parties—such as California's Middle Class Party, Rock & Roll Party, or Birthday Party—in your voter file. In other states (e.g., Indiana and Illinois), individuals select a party ballot when they opt to vote in a partisan primary. This allows you to create a party affiliation by looking at the individual's primary voting history. Finally, some states (e.g., Minnesota and Wisconsin) provide no meaningful party information.

School finance campaigns often begin with two assumptions. First, everyone supports the local schools. Second, parents are registered and will vote in the district's school finance election. Both are false. School elections fail nationwide because there are people who will vote "no" regardless of the nature and merit of the proposal. Parents also present a challenge. Not only are parents *not* always registered to vote, but even if they are registered, they easily forget to vote in school finance elections. Therefore, even the most basic annotated voter file should identify the registered voters in the district who have children in school. This annotation is developed by comparing the names and addresses of the parents in the district with the names and addresses of the community's registered voters. Furthermore, identifying registered parents enables the district to understand the parents' role in determining the school finance election's outcome. Armed with voting history data, the district can also determine how many of the registered parents have strong, vigorous voting records.

Equally valuable information includes voters in households with a recent district graduate, a donor to a school district education foundation or parent association, and parents of preschool-age children. If a district has been on the ballot previously, it is extremely important that its "past supporters" be identified in the current election's voter file.

There are also times when information developed for use by America's retail marketers should be added to basic voter file data. This need arises in states like Wisconsin where the voter files available from the state provide minimal information about the registered voters in a community. It also arises when a district faces a particularly difficult election environment and "microtargeting" to the extent the voter file will allow is necessary.

The residential address can be used to identify many of the consumer characteristics of the voters at that address. Homeowner status can be annotated, allowing one to identify those voters who are renters and those who own their own home. Length of residence, individual and household income, and education level can be added. Moreover, the last name of each voter can be used to add ethnic coding to the file. It is also possible to use the voter's full name and address to append e-mail addresses to the file. Finally, a file can be annotated by identifying such things as individuals who have hunting or fishing licenses, people who make donations to environmental or community groups, or the recreational activities in which someone in the household participates.

The most sophisticated level of annotation is the coding of each household according to its demographic and lifestyle characteristics. There are a number of these file segmentation systems available. The one we have applied to the art and science of winning school finance elections is the PRIZM NE system developed by Claritas. This system assigns each household to one of 66 different demographic groups. It allows one to code a file so that voters can be assigned to one of 14 social groups and to one of 11 life-stage groups.

All of this may sound very Orwellian but it does serve a very simple purpose as a district prepares for a school finance election. When combined with the results of a scientific random sample survey, all of the annotations added to a voter file allow for the development of very precise targets within the voting population. More important, once a file is fully annotated, microtargets can be developed within those targets, allowing for very focused voter contact.

Beyond identifying specific individuals and households in the voter file, U.S. Census data can be used to enhance the file. Valuable information (e.g., median household age, median household income, ethnic and racial background, median home value, and educational attainment) can bolster a campaign's database. To link these data to the voter file, the file must be "geocoded," a process that assigns a census tract or block group number to every address (or as many as technology will allow). Once you know the block group for a specific address, you can link the voter file at the block group level to census data. Such a link will not tell you definitively that an individual is in a specific income bracket or of a specific ethic group. It could, however, tell you whether you are dealing with a voter in a high-income or low-income neighborhood.

Finally, linking the voter file to the records of property value that are generally available from the county assessor allows you to separate properties with high or low assessed values as well as to more accurately identify rental properties. Assessor's data can be expensive, but there are times (especially in a bond election where the tax impact on each voter is based on their home's assessed value) when it is worth it.

"Counting" is the end product of the voter file preparation process. Once you have annotated the file as completely as possible, you will want to produce a *count book*. A count book quantifies all of the demographic features in the file. It provides the district and the campaign with a quick reference tool designed to better understand how many voters are, for example, male, parents, older than 65, or younger than 34.

How Do I Use a Count Book?

Assume for a moment we are in a school district that was able to build a voter file in which it identified current district parents, preschool parents, and the households from which students recently graduated. It has used this electronic file to generate a count book—a hardcopy record of all the annotations added to the voter file. This is an example of how this hypothetic district would use its count book to plan an election.

The count book tells the campaign that there are 2,450 current parents living in 1,225 households. Furthermore, it says phone numbers are available for 93 percent of these parent households. In addition, there are 1,004 preschool parents living in 502 households and 1,234 voters living in 616 households in which a student graduated from high school during the last five years. In both of these groups, the count book says that there are phone numbers available for 90 percent of the households.

All of these numbers allow the campaign to effectively plan to send a piece of direct mail to these groups followed by a phone canvass. First, add all of the households in all three groups. A mailing to parents, preschool parents, and the parents of recent graduates will involve 2,343 pieces of mail. If the campaign assumes that it will spend 75¢ per piece to print and mail the material it wants to provide to this audience, it now knows that it will cost $1,757.25 to execute this step in its campaign plan.

Next, the campaign can plan its phone canvass. Based on the information in the count book, there are approximately 2,100 phone numbers available for this audience. If the campaign assumes a volunteer can complete 15 canvass calls per hour and each volunteer will call for two hours a night, it knows that it will take 10 volunteers seven nights to call all 2,100 of these households.

Count books are generally organized so that the first page or "top sheet" presents counts for the file's important demographic features. Each subsequent page provides a similar complete demographic count for each individual demographic feature. Therefore, if the top sheet's first two lines tell you how many voters are male and how many are female, the second page will provide a complete demographic picture of the district's male voters while the third page will provide the same data for the district's female voters. All data in the count book are essential to the campaign's planning and execution process and integral to the key strategies of voter identification, canvassing, targeted communications, and get-out-the vote efforts.

NOTES

Portions of this chapter are reprinted with permission from the May 2009 issue of *School Business Affairs*. Copyright 2009 Association of School Business Officials. All rights reserved.

1. The process of ordering data from state or county offices varies from state to state and often from county to county. Increasingly, all of the information needed will be available on a Web site. In many cases, however, someone will need to visit an elections office, fill out the paperwork requesting voter data, and pick the data up when they are ready.
2. You cannot see how an individual voted, but you can tell when they voted.
3. The voting district or precinct may also be called a ward, a beat, or a box.

3

Looking Back to Plan Forward

In promoting its prime-time television hit *Crossing Jordan*, NBC touted star Jill Hennessy as "a sexy, smart, and fearless Boston medical examiner with a penchant for going beyond the call of duty to investigate crimes." A large fan base of forensic groupies tuned in weekly to watch Jordan "channel her inner anger toward piecing together complex murder cases that have been hidden, shoved aside—or conveniently forgotten," as the network put it. Rival CBS followed with the forensic blockbuster *CSI: Crime Scene Investigation*. In both cases, solving crimes required that clues first be coaxed from the dead and reassembled to understand what actually happened. Albeit not as sexy, school leaders also must be smart and fearless as they conduct their forensic studies—in this context at the examination table of school elections past.

Research and practice have yet to yield a modus operandi in K–12 education that always produces winners on school tax proposals. Whether it's bricks or mortar or requests for more operating money, each election type and context are unique, with no guarantee that a set of campaign strategies—even if previously successful in another district—won't fail in your community. If successful campaigns were not such a delicate balance of science and art, the formula for success would have long since been discovered, resulting in significantly more school districts finding success at the polls. This reality aside, both research and successful practice suggest the best way to start planning your next successful facility or operating referendum is to take a much closer look at your last.

REARVIEW MIRROR

Most school districts squander a key strategic opportunity when they fail to collect, analyze, and archive valuable data after school finance elections—equally important whether a campaign succeeds or fails. The most obvious data analysis, although seldom done well, is to understand who participated in a recent school referendum in comparison to earlier elections. How did the campaign effort in support of the ballot question influence the electorate? How did various demographic groups vote relative to their proportionate share of the voter file as well as past voting habits? To what extent did targeted supporters show up from various precincts or attendance areas? These are examples of the questions that can be answered during a post-election analysis, yielding critical information for school leaders who are planning future campaigns.

Lessons from the Past

There are basic questions that need to be asked during a post-election analysis. The answers to these questions form the "lesson" for planners of your next election.

- What type of election just occurred?
- When might this type of election occur again?
- Did parents participate in this school finance election?
- If parent participation was not uniform, are there parent groups that will need a little extra attention during the next election?
- Did identified nonparent supporters participate?
- What can the next campaign learn from the participation of nonparent supporters?
- Are there areas of the district that present unique challenges to the next campaign? The characteristics of these areas and the attitudes of the voters who live in them should be explored with maps and surveys.

The idea that a school district should look back at its last election when planning the next election is based on the concept that the best predictors of future voting behavior are the past actions of those voters. Therefore, understanding the key factors and behaviors in past local elections (e.g., older voters, female voters, or voters living in certain areas) will help a district plan a successful election.

A post-election analysis begins by isolating all of the voter file information about the population that voted in the district's most recent election. Once this population is isolated, all of its demographic characteristics are counted and compared to the population of all voters in the district. Specifically, we want to know which demographic groups are overrepresented or underrepresented in this population.

For example, the counts developed to identify the number of male and female voters that cast ballots are used to calculate the percentage of the total number of voters who participated who are male versus female. These percentages are then compared to the entire voter file. This process is repeated for each significant demographic feature. A typical result might show that although women make up 52 percent of all registered voters in the district, post-election research finds that women made up 56 percent of the population that voted. The district now knows that its last election attracted more women than men.

Knowing the election attracted more women allows us to ask additional questions. Were these older or younger women? How many of these women have school-age children? Do these women have a long-term history of voting in every local election or do they generally not vote? Each detail is a clue that allows us to create a picture of what happened on election day. That picture, in turn, serves as a road map for the district's next school finance election.

What about the men in the district? If men are underrepresented in the population that voted, we want to ask all the same questions to determine the characteristics of male voters who missed this election. In one specific case, a post-election analysis found that a large number of the men who did not vote were younger parents with relatively weak voting histories. While their wives had gotten to the polls to vote for the school finance proposal, these potential parent "yes" votes failed to cast a ballot. This information allowed the district to add a new element—a male mentor program to help remind fathers to vote—to its next campaign plan. As part of the program, a team of older male parents with long-term voting records worked throughout the campaign to communicate directly with younger dads. At each step, they emphasized the need not only to support the school district's proposal as a volunteer but also to vote "yes" on election day. An analysis of the campaign results confirmed that it worked. Not only did turnout among younger male parents increase significantly, but the district also turned a heartbreaking loss into a solid win.

Once a profile of the voting population has been developed, a post-election analysis turns to look in detail at the election day performance of two groups—those who were identified as supporters of the district's proposal among all registered voters and those who were identified among parents.[1] Each group needs to be examined in two ways:

- How was each group represented on election day?
- Did most of the people in each group cast a ballot?

In both groups, overrepresentation is extremely important. For example, if parents represent 23 percent of the registered voter population, they are overrepresented if we find they comprised 36 percent of the population that voted on election day. In all cases, we want to find parents overrepresented in a school finance election. This is the result of two factors that exist in almost every school finance election. First, parents should be naturally attracted to a school finance election. Second, every school finance campaign must have a program designed to maximize the parent vote. Therefore, if parents are underrepresented in the population that voted on election day, either there was a serious flaw in the planning or execution of the campaign or the district's proposal was significantly out of alignment with the priorities of the parent population. Any district that finds itself in this situation has some major work ahead—work which must be completed before considering another school finance election.

Even when parents are overrepresented in the population that voted, the district needs to look at the degree to which the potential vote within the parent population was "maximized." For example, if parents represent 23 percent of the voter file but comprise 36 percent of the population that voted, an initial conclusion could be that parent participation in the election was strong. But if only 43 percent of all registered parents took the time to cast a ballot, this initial conclusion would be wrong. Leaving 57 percent of the parent population at home on election day means the campaign failed to maximize the parent vote. Such a situation can easily make the difference between an election day win and an election day loss.

Knowing that parent participation might be a problem allows the district's next effort to structure its campaign plan to address this challenge. Where absentee voting is easy, campaigns often plan to make sure all supportive parents with weak voting histories "vote by mail" long before election day. Such campaigns may even include the preprinting of an absentee ballot application so the recipient only needs to sign the form and wait for their ballot to arrive in the mail. Other campaigns have developed extensive "buddy systems." Similar to the male mentor program, parents who can be counted on to vote are assigned a number of election buddies (i.e., parents without solid voting records). Throughout the campaign, these parents systematically contact their "buddies" to emphasize the importance of every vote.

Using a Postmortem to Target Future Voters

The results of a post-election analysis often cause a district to modify the way in which voters are targeted in the next campaign. For example, a large school district placed a bond proposal on the ballot and then executed an extremely weak communications effort. As a result, the bond proposal failed to win voter support. In a post-election analysis, it became very clear that only one-third of the parent population had voted in this election.

In their second effort, parents were divided into two target groups. Group #1 was made up of those parents who, despite a weak communications effort, found out that a bond was on the ballot and voted. Group #2 comprised those parents who did not vote in the first election. Instead of incurring the cost of increasing the amount of mail and telephone contact made with all parents, the second campaign was able to focus an increased amount of contact where it was needed most—on the parents in Group #2. This group of parents received two to three times as much mail as the first group and was the focus of more telephone contact by campaign volunteers. The result was a large increase in parent participation and a win on election day.

A post-election analysis also involves a careful look at the nonparent voters identified by the campaign as supporting the district's finance proposal. Though many techniques can be used to identify supporters who are not parents, all rely on campaign volunteers asking community members if they will support the proposal. In successful campaigns, this is not a random contact program. Specific portions of the nonparent population are targeted for contact by the campaign. After election day, it is important to look at how well this population performed and, in turn, evaluate the effectiveness of the campaign's targeting effort. Are identified supporters overrepresented or underrepresented in the population that voted? What percentage of the total number of identified supporters cast ballots? As with the parent population, identified supporters may be overrepresented in the population that voted but the campaign may not be satisfied with the actual percentage casting ballots. Results can vary greatly. We have seen results ranging from a dismal 33 percent of supporters participating in the election up to an outstanding 95 percent of identified support casting ballots.

Especially when the potential in this population is not maximized on election day, analysis provides the needed information to craft a more effective campaign plan. By looking at the gender, age, party affiliation, and geographic location of identified supporters, such an analysis will allow you to develop a clear picture of the individuals who failed to cast ballots. For example, if such an analysis reveals that all younger identified supporters who were Democrats with a weak long-term voting record failed to vote in your election, this fact will help the next campaign target its volunteer resources more effectively.

Voting by Area

Surprising differences can be found when elections are compared. A post-election analysis completed for a Minnesota school district revealed that one part of the district voted only when the school placed a proposal on the ballot with a gubernatorial or presidential election. Like many school districts in the country, their school district boundaries are not contiguous with the city boundaries. The area of the district where the level of voter participation varied from election to election was part of a city identified with another school district. Without a vigorous effort to communicate with these voters, they would not understand that their votes made a difference to a school district they believed served another community. Since the post-election analysis for this district was completed as it prepared to place a proposal on the ballot with the election of the governor, district leaders modified their voter contact program to make sure these voters were provided with enough information to make it clear which school district served their neighborhoods—and which school district needed their votes.

A number of campaigns have developed extensive plans to maximize the "yes" votes cast by recent school district graduates. These young voters are very often still registered in the community although they may be living on a college campus, a military base, or in an apartment. They can usually be identified in the voter file by combining their age with the fact that they are still associated with a parent household due to the presence of a younger sibling. These campaigns often work with these young adults during the summer or winter break to inform them of the importance of their vote in the district's upcoming election. This effort may also extend to Facebook or Twitter as a way to say in touch even when these potential supporters are out of the district. Post-election analysis of the votes cast by these younger voters will determine if this campaign tactic works. When it does, it should be included in the next campaign. When it does not, it should be replaced with a more effective tactic.

Finally, a post-election analysis should examine how the election you just held compares to other recent elections. Too many school districts make the assumption that all elections are alike. They are not. Each election has a character that is defined by the types of candidates or issues that appear on the ballot. For example, a November election for a governor or the president will attract a much younger, more male population than a primary, school board, or special election. The latter generally will attract a population that is older, more female, and more likely to vote in any election held in the area. Therefore, if your district just held a very successful school finance election on the ballot with the gubernatorial election, do not assume that you will be able to apply the same campaign plan to your next election if it is being held on a special election ballot.

One of the biggest differences among elections is the level of turnout. Despite all of the concern surrounding declining presidential election turnout during the last 50 years, a presidential election will attract the highest level of turnout in most communities, typically in the 70–80 percent range. A gubernatorial election, if it appears on a different ballot, will typically draw 50–60 percent of registered voters. There is generally a much lower level of voter participation in all other elections, such as nominating primaries, city council, or school board elections, which are often in the 30–40 percent range. These election characteristics always need to be verified in your district. The likely size and demography of the turnout has a direct bearing on the number of voters you need to draw to the polls to be successful.

PLANNING AHEAD BY LOOKING BACK

The purpose of looking back, of course, is to determine what happened and why. The foundation for success at the ballot box begins with an examination of what happened during prior elections conducted within the district. Like medical examiners in *Crossing Jordan* and *CSI*, successful school leaders need to piece together disconnected clues about voter behavior, demographic tendencies, and turnout under various conditions. Reconstructing this puzzle, in combination with other steps in a comprehensive planning model, provides the foundation for an effective campaign and guides the critical steps of voter identification and a get-out-the-vote effort, which are key ingredients to achieving success in your next finance election.

NOTE

1. This information is extremely important and is often poorly stored or discarded as soon as the polls have closed. Every election should generate an electronic file of its identified supporters, containing sufficient information (e.g., name, address, phone number, and state voter identification number) to enable it to be easily linked to a new copy of the voter file used in a future election campaign.

Mapping

If a picture is truly worth a thousand words, a good set of demographic maps is worth thousands of columns of numbers, counts, and statistics. Simply put, the statistics defining a school district can be made much easier to read and understand when they are visually displayed in a set of demographic maps. As part of the school finance election planning process, the results of the district's last finance election, the demographic characteristics of local voters, *and* U.S. Census data should be used to visually explore the nature and character of the district's neighborhoods and communities. The maps created as part of this process clearly and quickly enable school leaders to see the characteristics that may cause a proposal to be received in very different ways in various parts of the district.

This chapter examines three types of maps:

- *Election maps.* These maps extend the process of a post-election analysis. They are created from election results and the information contained in a fully annotated voter file.
- *U.S. Census data maps.* These maps build on election data by using information available from the U.S. Census to explore the demographic characteristics of the entire community.
- *Practical maps.* These maps help a campaign plan and execute parts of its voter contact program.

ELECTION MAPS

Precinct-by-precinct election results were not discussed as part of a post-election analysis. Precinct results can reveal whether support for the district's last proposal was uniform or varied from neighborhood to neighborhood. If support was not uniform, it is important to identify not only those areas in which the proposal did well but also those in which it was soundly defeated. Most important, the district needs to identify those precincts where a few additional votes cast for or against the proposal would have changed the outcome of the vote at the precinct level.

To illustrate, let us look at the results of an election in which a school finance proposal won with 51.8 percent of the vote. Table 4.1 presents the precinct-by-precinct results as they were provided to the district after the

Table 4.1.   Precinct-by-Precinct Results

Precinct name	Percentage Yes
Arnold	53.0
Deeds 1	54.3
Deeds 2	51.1
Douglas	54.1
Easttown	51.1
Edgerville 1	42.7
Edgerville 2	54.5
Edgerville 3	52.1
James 1	41.0
James 2	41.8
Liberty 1	51.3
Liberty 2	56.2
Liberty 3	53.4
Liberty 4	51.2
Lincoln 1	53.8
Lincoln 2	55.4
Madison 1	55.4
Madison 2	51.0
Madison 3	53.2
Madison 4	54.5
Madison 5	55.6
Upper James	50.1
Washington 1	53.7
Washington 2	42.1
Washington 3	58.3
Westboro	53.1
Wilderness	53.6

election was certified by the local elections office. These results make it clear that the district's school finance proposal did extremely well in precincts such as Washington 3 and Liberty 2, where it won with more than 56 percent of the vote. These numbers also make it clear that in precincts James 1 and James 2, the district's proposal was beaten badly—winning only 41 percent of the vote. These numbers, however, reveal neither where these areas are located within the district nor anything about the voting and demographic characteristics of the people who live in these precincts. Mapping these results will allow the district to see immediately where these areas are located. By mapping additional data, the district gains a clearer view of the voters and why they voted against the district's school finance proposal.

Mapping precinct results reveals that three of the precincts that voted "no"—James 1, James 2, and Edgerville 1—are on the district's eastern end. The fourth, Washington 2, is in the south-central part of the district. On map 4.1, these precincts are depicted as black areas. There are also a number of precincts that create a band across the district from east to

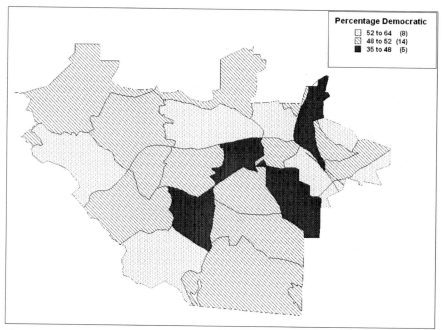

Map 4.1.   Yes Percentage

west where the proposal narrowly won or lost. These areas on the map are shaded with diagonal lines. In the remainder of the district, the proposal did very well.

To understand why the district's proposal did so poorly in these precincts, the district must look at other voter file data. Since this district had a fully annotated voter file available during its last election, it can calculate the portion of each precinct represented by registered parents. The results of these calculations can be used to create a map illustrating the areas of the district where parents represent a large percentage of the voting population and the areas where they represent a small percentage of the population registered to vote. A map using this information shows the four precincts where the district's proposal received its lowest level of support are also the areas where there is the lowest concentration of registered parents. The areas across the middle of the district where the outcome of the election was close are all areas where the parent population is neither a very large nor a very small percentage of the voting population. On map 4.2, areas where the parents represent less than 10

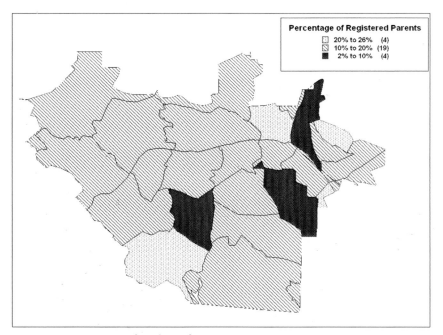

Map 4.2.   Percentage of Registered Parents

percent of the registered voters in the precinct are printed in black. Areas where the parents represent more that 20 percent of the voting population are shaded gray with white stripes.

Continuing to use the available voter file information, the district can look at the party affiliation of voters in each precinct.[1] Map 4.3 illustrates the percentage of the voting population for each precinct that are registered members of the Democratic Party. Although school finance proposals are not partisan proposals and receive support from all types of voters, it is generally true that voters who are affiliated with the Democratic Party are more likely to vote for a proposal than are their Republican neighbors. Therefore, knowing where the Democrats are concentrated will expand the campaign's understanding of the finance election's outcome. The areas printed in black are where Democrats make up less than 48 percent of the population of registered voters. There are five of these areas, and four are precincts in which the finance proposal received its lowest level of support. As a result, the district can begin to conclude that a lack of registered parents as well as a lack of Democrats may have

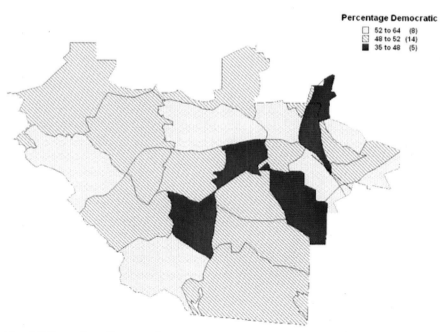

Percentage Democratic

☐ 52 to 64 (8)
▨ 48 to 52 (14)
■ 35 to 48 (5)

Map 4.3 Percentage Democratic

made a difference in the way a particular precinct voted on the district's most recent proposal.

An additional type of map available to the campaign uses the classification of voters according to their past election activity, which was discussed in chapter 2. The classifications are:

- *Very Active Voters*—individuals who almost never miss an election.
- *Active Voters*—individuals who get to most elections.
- *Less Active or New Voters*—those individuals who either vote very infrequently or have recently registered to vote.

On map 4.4, the percentage of the voting population in each precinct that consists of Very Active Voters has been used to illustrate where voting will be heaviest and lightest in any local election. The areas printed in black represent the areas in the district where Very Active Voters represent less than 10 percent of the voting population. The areas shaded with white stripes on gray background are where more than 20 percent of the

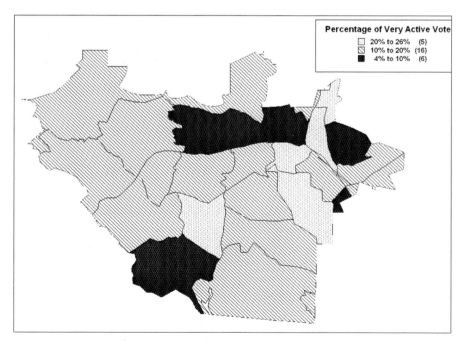

Map 4.4 Percentage of Very Active Voters

voting population is a Very Active Voter. The four precincts in which the district's school finance proposal received the lowest level of support are all precincts with a high percentage of Very Active Voters. This information expands our understanding of the voters in these precincts. It also tells the district that the attitudes of these voters will have an impact on any future district election. Because they are active voters and they now have a history of voting against a local school finance proposal, the district may need to look for a way to build a better base of support among these individuals before its next election.

CENSUS DATA MAPS

To build a better base of support with the voters in the four precincts in which support for the last school finance proposal was weakest, it is important to learn more about these individuals. To do so, data from the U.S. Census can be mapped. The U.S. Census contains a vast amount of information about the residents of every community. The data can be mapped by using any of the geographic definitions developed for the census. In maps 4.5, 4.6, and 4.7, data will be mapped into the census block groups contained inside the school district—beginning with age.

Map 4.5 illustrates the median age for each block group as measured by the census.[2] The areas printed in black represent areas where the median age is older than 50. There are four of these areas. One corresponds to Edgerville 1, which is one of the precincts in which the last school finance election fared very poorly. The other three are in precincts in which the proposal did well. Therefore, although age may be a factor in explaining why the last proposal did poorly in Edgerville 1, it is not the whole answer. Because there are areas in the district where older residents appear to have supported the school district, it may be possible for the district to find older supporters in those precincts who might be willing to help emphasize the importance of the schools to the older voters in Edgerville 1. An endorsement from other older voters might reduce the inclination of the residents of Edgerville 1 to oppose school taxes.

To continue to explore the district's demography, one can consult a map that illustrates the median household income in the block groups that make up the model school district. On map 4.6, the areas printed in black

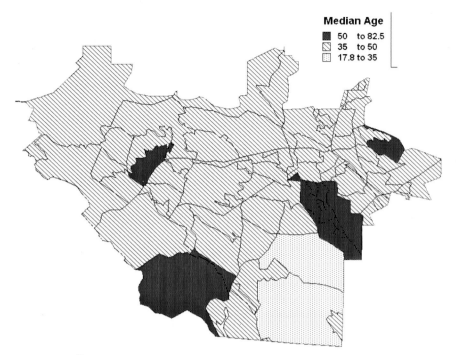

Median Age
- 50 to 82.5
- 35 to 50
- 17.8 to 35

Map 4.5 Median Age

represent the district areas where the median household income is lowest (less than $50,000 per year). The areas shaded in light gray represent areas where the median household income is highest (from $76,000 to $295,000 per year). Three of the areas with a low median household income are contained in Edgerville 1, James 1, and James 2—precincts in which the school finance election did very poorly. Combining what was learned from this map and the map illustrating median age, it can be concluded that in Edgerville 1 the proposal did very poorly in part because older, less-affluent individuals populate the precinct. These individuals are also not Democrats or parents but vote all of the time.

Finally, the district can map the median assessed value of homes in a district. Map 4.7 reveals that most of the district is very homogenous, and most property is assessed at more than $308,000. Two precincts, however, contain areas where the assessed value is much lower. The portions printed in black represent areas where the median assessed value of residential property is lowest (less than $204,000). The areas printed in darker gray represent block groups where the median assessed value is between

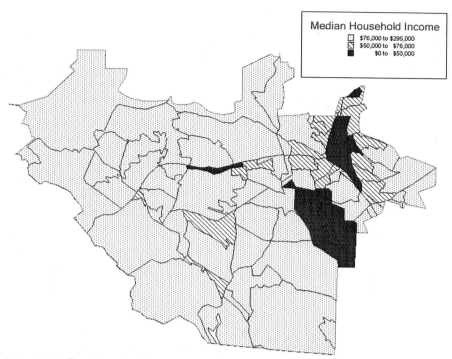

Map 4.6 Median Household Income

$204,000 and $308,000. The areas where the median assessed value is less than $204,000 correspond to two of the precincts—Edgerville 1 and James 2—in which the district's proposal did poorly. Using these maps, the district can build a fairly complete demographic profile of the district residents who will represent the "toughest sell" when the next school finance proposal is placed on the ballot.

This discussion of demographic mapping started with the results of a previous school finance election and used maps created from voter file and U.S. Census data to learn more about the nature of the voters who opposed the last proposal. Maps using voter file and U.S. Census data can also be used to plan a future school finance election even when there are no results available from a previous election. In the maps created for this chapter from voter file and U.S. Census data, it was revealed that four precincts—Edgerville 1, James 1, James 2, and Washington 2—have demographic and voting characteristics that define them as different from

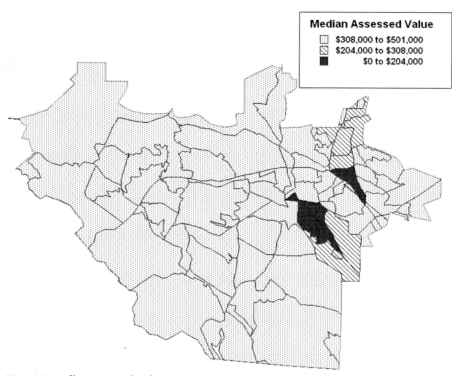

Map 4.7 Median Assessed Value

Table 4.2.   District Precinct Characteristics

Precinct	Percent parent	Percent Democrats	% Very Active Voters	Median Age	Median Assessed Value	Median Household Income
James 1	Low	Low	High	Middle range	Middle range	Middle range-Low
James 2	Low	Low	High	Middle range	Middle range – Low	Low
Edgerville 1	Low	Low	High	High	Middle range – Low	Low
Washington 2	Low	Low	High	Middle range	High	Middle range-High

the rest of the district. Even without a knowledge of how anyone in the district might vote on a proposal, a table summarizing the characteristics of the district's precincts allows the district to see the characteristics these four precincts have in common—characteristics that also define them as a region populated by individuals different than those in the rest of the district.

Knowing these regions exist before a community survey is completed will allow survey results to explore in detail regional differences in opinion concerning a school finance proposal. If the survey demonstrates that some of the areas with unique demographic characteristics also present a campaign with some unique challenges, plans can be developed to make sure these neighborhoods receive special attention from the campaign.

PRACTICAL MAPS

The maps discussed up to this point all allow the district to increase its knowledge of the whole district. They provide global pictures of the district's characteristics. Practical maps, however, generally present detailed information about a precinct or a section of a precinct. They are used to help make sure everyone in the campaign knows how to find each polling place. In addition, they can be very useful as voter contact efforts—for example, a community walk, a "dear friend" campaign,[3] or a get-out-the-vote drive—are planned.

The simplest practical map illustrates where the polling place will be in each precinct. Such maps can be very useful as volunteers work to ensure voters know where to go on election day. Because they simply provide information and do not advocate for a "yes" or "no" vote, these maps can also be posted at school, where parents and teachers can use them to help get voters to the ballot box. Map 4.8 illustrates this type of practical map.

This type of map can also be an effective planning tool for campaign activities. Many campaigns include a community walk during which volunteers go door to door to make contact with likely supporters who cannot be reached by phone. To plan this type of walk, a precinct map depicting where these voters live can be very useful. Map 4.9 places a little flag at each address where an uncontacted, registered parent lives.

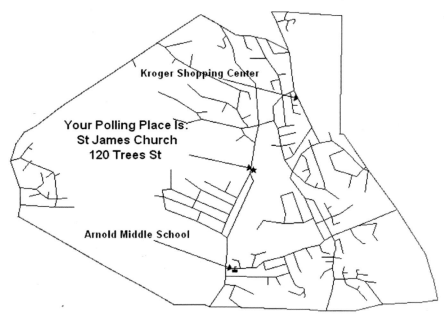

Map 4.8 Polling Place

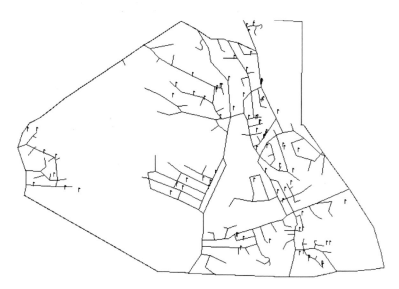

Map 4.9 Voter Contact Map

As street names are not assigned in alphabetical order, those charged with the task of planning a walk to these houses can use such a map to group streets that are connected and close together. A similar map could be created showing where all the identified "yes" voters live in the precinct. As a campaign plans its get-out-the-vote drive, such a map would allow it to determine in advance the best way for every "yes" voter to get to the polls on election day.

Campaign volunteers can also use maps to decide where it is practical to walk to all of the parent doors in the precinct. Map 4.10 zooms into one corner of the precinct. It is clear that a door-to-door walk on Ruppel Place could be very productive while there will be no need to walk down Rohrer Drive. The level of detail that can be achieved on such a planning map can be increased tremendously.

The last sample map in this chapter examines one city block. On map 4.11, homes shaded gray are the homes of public school parents. The presence of a gray dot indicates the presence of a registered parent. A black dot represents a registered parent who voted in the last election. This type of map makes it easy to visually explore the information that is presented in the numbers found in a count book. Where the count book may have indicated that the registered voters in this city block were older

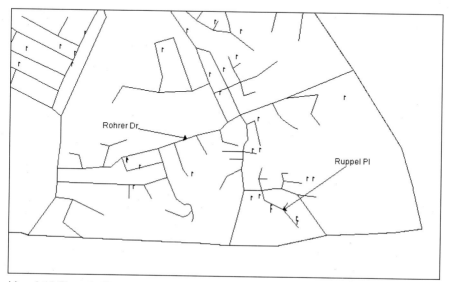

Map 4.10 Door-to-Door Map

602	601	600	601	311 1	601
		604	605	610	
608	609	608	611		609
614	615	612	613	612	613
618	619	616	617	618	619
620	623	620	621	620	
624	625		625	624	625
	629	624		628	629
632	633		629	632	631
		632		636	
636	637		637		637
		640	641	640	
644	645	644	645	644	645
648	649	648	649	648	651
		652	653	654	
658	657	656	655	658	657

Map 4.11. Single City Block

than voters in other parts of the district, the map allows us to easily see that this "graying" effect may reflect the fact that many of the parents in this area are not registered. Of the 17 households where a parent has been identified, six have no one registered to vote. In three other parent households, only one parent is registered. The lack of black dots also makes it very clear that this is a neighborhood where a stronger get-out-the-vote effort will be needed in any future election. Only two parent voters got to the polls in the last district election.

Mapping large areas of the district in this way allows those planning a school finance election to see clearly and quickly where there are concentrations of shaded parent households. Likewise, the grey and black dots make it very easy to see where a campaign will need to concentrate on voter registration and get-out-the-vote efforts. The information available from such a map can be expanded. It is also possible to map the houses on a street where parents live and then differentiate the houses in which the parents are Very Active Voters from those in which the parents are Less Active or New Voters. This type of map can also be developed during a campaign, allowing campaign leadership to better plan door-to-door voter contact.

NOTES

1. In many states, voters do not register by party. In those states, you can use precinct-level results for minor statewide offices to identify the partisan character of a precinct. (Note: Minor statewide offices are those elected positions that never seem to attract a lot of media attention and in which the candidates involved are not well known even by election day. In fact, in many of these races, only the candidate's immediate family really knows for whom they are voting.)

2. Very good annual U.S. Census updates are also available. These can be obtained from the Census Bureau's Web site (www.census.gov) or purchased from commercial data companies such as Claritas or, in some cases, obtained from local planning offices. These updates are essential when mapping data five or six years after the U.S. Census was taken.

3. To conduct a "dear friend" campaign, campaign volunteers handwrite postcards to supportive voters in their neighborhoods who might forget to vote when the district has a school finance proposal on the ballot.

5

Community Survey

A community survey is a scientific measurement of voter opinion at a specific moment in time that is designed to determine if it is feasible to place a school finance proposal on the ballot. If it is feasible, the survey determines how much the community is willing to increase local taxes for the benefit of the schools. In addition, such a survey functions as an assessment of the school district's performance and should explore the community's perception of the overall quality of the education being provided to local children, the ability of the district to manage its budget, and the degree to which voters believe the district spends tax dollars wisely. In most states, school districts are allowed to commission and pay for such a survey as part of the school finance election preparation process. In every election, it is essential that a community survey be completed before a proposal is placed on the ballot.

THE BASICS: WHO?

Every school finance election survey should be based on interviews with registered voters.[1] In every community, the most active registered voters in the school district will have a very strong influence on the success or failure of any proposal placed on the ballot. Therefore, understanding how these voters react to a proposal is extremely important. When a community survey is based on interviews with registered voters, it also extends the demographic knowledge gained by reading the count book produced from the contents of the district's voter file. Likewise, it adds depth to the understanding developed about voter behavior by a post-election analysis. But a community survey achieves these goals only if it is based on interviews with registered voters.

Important Terms

The following terms are used in this chapter and may be unfamiliar.

- *Cross-tabulation*—dividing the responses according to the demographic characteristics of the individuals being interviewed; often called "cross-tabs." The simplest is the cross-tab by gender that allows one to look at the response among male voters separated from the response among female voters.
- *Uninformed benchmark*—a question included in surveys before detailed information is presented to those being interviewed about the need for and cost of a district's proposal.
- *Informed benchmark*—a question included in the survey after information has been presented to those being interviewed.
- *Margin of error*—a measure of the accuracy of the results of the survey.
- *Sample*—the list of individuals who may be asked to complete an interview as part of the survey process. These individuals are selected at random from all of the voters in the district.
- *Sample size*—the number of completed interviews used as the basis for a survey.

Saying that a survey will be based on interviews with registered voters does not answer all of the questions involved in deciding *who* should be interviewed. There are a number of ways to design the sample for such a community survey. All have been used to plan successful school finance elections, but each has some distinct strengths and weaknesses.

Some polls are based only on interviews with the most active voters in the community. Using the definitions developed in the discussion of the voter file in chapter 2, a sample is designed that will cause all of the interviews to be completed with Very Active Voters. Because these voters will have a major impact on any election held in the district, this approach will produce the safest recommendations for the district. But this approach may also provide the district with recommendations that raise a minimal amount of money, since the most active voters in most districts are older voters without school-age children.

Other polls are based only on interviews with the voters that the count book says are most likely to participate in an election scheduled for the next date available for a proposal. This approach produces recommendations that are extremely accurate as long as the assumptions made about who will probably vote in the next election are not changed by events that occur between the execution of the survey and election day. If events do force a change in those assumptions, the results of such a survey may not provide as much insight into the impact of those changes or allow the district to effectively explore the feasibility of placing a proposal on any of the other election dates available in the future.

Finally, some polls involve interviews with voters of all types after excluding individuals from the sample who have died, moved, or stopped voting. This type of survey will produce the most complete picture of community reaction to a school finance election. In addition, the potential for success or failure in a number of election environments can be explored. Cross-tabulation is used to explore the reaction of the Very Active Voters in the district and to explore the support available from those most likely to vote in the next available election date. If there is little or no support for a tax increase among the most active voters in the community or among the voters most likely to participate in the next available election date, the picture of voter opinion developed in this type of survey will allow the district to assess the benefits and risks involved with a proposal that must depend on voters who will need to be vigorously reminded to vote if the proposal is to succeed. The disadvantage of this type of survey is that the margin of error among many of the groups of voters interviewed is higher.

THE BASICS: HOW MANY?

A community survey does not involve calls to all voters in the district. In fact, these surveys are based on interviews with a relatively small number of registered voters. Deciding how many interviews to complete as part of a community survey depends on two factors. The first relates to the fact that the primary goal of the survey is to measure overall community opinion with a sufficient level of precision to predict the feasibility of a school finance election. The level of precision or the margin of error in any survey is determined by a formula that is based on the total number of interviews completed for the survey. It does not depend on the total number of registered voters in the school district. As noted by Celina Lake, "A sample of 200 from a congressional district has the same error rate as a sample of 200 drawn from the United States" (Lake and Callbeck Harper, 1987). Therefore, we recommend a community survey be based on a minimum of 300 interviews, achieving a margin of error of ±5.5 percent with a 95 percent confidence level. In general, sample sizes tend to range from 300 to 600 interviews. Such surveys present results where the margin of error is ±5.5 percent for 300 interviews to ±4 percent for 600 interviews. This level of precision is sufficient to plan a successful school finance election.[2]

The second factor involved in determining an appropriate sample size applies in districts with large voting populations and in which the results of a post-election analysis or demographic mapping have made it clear that the survey should also be designed to accurately measure regional differences of opinion. In such cases, the sample size might be increased to 800 or 1,000 to increase the level of precision in each region of the district.

An example will illustrate how and why this is done. A suburban school district in California's San Francisco Bay area is home to 70,000 voters in three distinct regions. One is composed of three small suburban communities where incomes and home values are significantly higher than in the rest of the district. The second is a larger suburban city that has a more diverse mixture of income levels and ethnic groups. It also includes a well-developed downtown business section in addition to its residential neighborhoods. The third region is a large retirement community where all residents must be older than 55 and no children are allowed. The distinct nature of each region is reflected in the district's count book, in the results of its post-election analysis, and in demographic mapping.

To ensure a survey can accurately measure differences of opinion concerning a school tax in each of these regions, the sample size in this district is routinely increased to 800. Completing this number of interviews increases the overall precision of the survey. More important, it allows the survey to include enough interviews in each region that the margin of error for each area is sufficient to allow opinion in the more upscale suburbs to be compared to opinion in the larger city. Opinion in both areas can then be compared with the reaction of the retirement community to a school finance election.

There are practical limits, however, to increasing the sample size in a community survey for a school district. Some districts are just too small. If there are only 2,500 to 3,500 voters in the district, it is not necessary—or practical—to complete more than 300 interviews. In districts with fewer than 15,000 voters, it may not be practical to complete more than 400 interviews. Attempting to do so will simply become disruptive and the persistence of the interview team could potentially anger local voters.

THE BASICS: HOW?

The interviews completed as a part of this type of survey are done via telephone. At this point, the phone has one major advantage over surveys completed through the mail or over the Internet. Before the first interview begins, the information in the count book has defined the demography of the district's voting population. As telephone interviews are completed, the demography of the interviewees is carefully monitored and adjustments are made to the selection of phone numbers from the sample to ensure the population interviewed has the same demographic characteristics as the population of voters in the district. If one is trying to interview through the mail or over the Internet, one can only hope that all demographic groups will respond.

The advantages offered by a telephone survey are changing, however. The advent of caller ID and the use of cell phones make telephone interviewing more difficult and expensive.[3] As the Internet continues to evolve, it offers more and more opportunities for interviewing. E-mail addresses can be appended to voter files so that an invitation to participate in a survey can be sent to specific voters. This will also allow for responses collected over the Internet to be matched to information in the voter file and made available for cross-tabulation. The limitation Internet interviewing poses is that e-mail addresses are not universally available. Nor will all voters respond in the same way to an invitation to participate in an Internet survey.

Despite this limitation, some of the companies that currently provide telephone interviewing services have begun to offer an interviewing process that blends an e-mail invitation with telephone interviewing. Voters for whom an e-mail address is available are invited to participate in a survey posted on the Internet. The demography of the voters who respond to this invitation and complete surveys is then checked against the demography of the voter file. Phone interviews are conducted with those demographic groups that did not respond.[4] As this and other innovative approaches to data collection are tried and their reliability evaluated, new tools will be available to replace telephone interviewing.

For the moment, however, the telephone is the most reliable tool available for school finance surveys. In addition, there is a secondary reason for relying on the telephone to complete the interviews required for a community survey. The telephone will be the primary means by which a campaign in support of a school finance election makes contact with local voters. If the survey can use the telephone to complete a set of interviews, and the results of the interviews demonstrate it is feasible to place a proposal on the ballot and expect to win, the campaign in support of that proposal can also expect to use the phone to identify enough support to win on election day.

THE BASICS: WHEN?

The timing of a community survey is a compromise between a desire to collect survey results as close to election day as possible and the need to use those results to plan and shape the district's proposal. In an ideal world, a district would execute a survey a few days before it had to place a school finance proposal on the ballot and have the results back just before the school board votes to call the election. The survey's results would reflect the attitudes of the voters in the district in an economic and political environment that would probably not change significantly before election day. Unfortunately, completing a survey just before the district must call an election does not allow the district to use the results to shape the proposal, plan the presentation of the proposal to the community, or thoughtfully assess the strengths and weaknesses of the projects to be funded by the school finance election. Therefore, community surveys are generally completed three to six months before the district must act to call an election. Timing the survey in this way affords the district enough time to react to all of the survey's information. Most importantly, the district can ensure that the projects it wants to fund by a tax increase will align well with the attitudes and opinions of those local voters.

There are also times when a district will plan for two surveys. This approach allows an initial survey to be completed 10–12 months before the district must act. These early surveys are used to explore the possible ways in which tax funds will be spent so projects can be developed in alignment with community opinion. An early survey will also identify projects that are out of alignment and require extensive community discussion if voters are to understand why and how these projects are important to the district's health and strength. Early surveys are also useful in districts in which recent events make it clear that local voters may have a less than positive opinion of the district's ability to plan or spend tax dollars wisely. By exploring voter opinion 10–12 months before the district must call an election, a communications plan can be developed addressing concerns among local voters about the district's fiscal skills and overall performance.

If an early survey is completed, a second (shorter) survey is generally planned just a few weeks or months before the district must place a proposal on the ballot. This survey will retest tax tolerance and assess the impact of any communication with local voters undertaken as a result of the first survey.

THE QUESTIONNAIRE

The community survey's questionnaire needs to test the impact of information about the district's school finance proposal on the level of support available in the community. School finance elections are different from all other elections because the only thing that can motivate an individual to vote to give away money is information about *why* the district needs the money. Other elections—even other referenda—do not have the kind of direct, immediate impact on household budgets that one finds in a school finance election. In a candidate race, many voters will make up their mind as soon as they find out the candidate is a Republican or a Democrat—or, in the case of the 2003 California gubernatorial recall election, a well-known actor and political "outsider." In a school tax election, the only party that exists is the uninformed party—voters who will vote "no" because they do not know anything (or enough) about the proposal. To understand clearly what information prevents this reaction and persuades voters to cast a "yes" vote, a community survey must test the impact of presenting voters with more and more information about the tax proposal.

The first step in the interview, therefore, is to ask everyone if they favor or oppose the district's proposal before any detailed information is presented. For a bond election, the question might read as follows: "The Brisbane Elementary School District may place a bond measure on the ballot that would increase property taxes to raise the funds needed to renovate the district's schools and classrooms. Would you favor or oppose such a proposal?" When the survey is designed to explore a tax increase to raise operating funds, the question might read: "The Stillwater Area Public Schools may ask local voters to approve an increase in local property taxes to provide the district with the funds needed to avoid budget cuts, the elimination of teaching positions, and an increase in class size. Would you favor or oppose such a proposal?"

This question is referred to as the *uninformed benchmark* (see figure 5.1). As these examples illustrate, these questions provide very few details about the proposal. The interviewee knows it involves an increase in local taxes. But the question does not present any information about the cost of the proposal to the individual being interviewed. The possible ways in which these funds will be used are described only in general terms. The purpose is to identify those voters who will support virtually anything the district places on the ballot. Identifying this population tells the district the size and demographic character of the base of support for its proposal.

Once the uninformed benchmark question has been asked, details about the district's proposal are presented. These questions attempt to break the whole proposal into its smallest component parts and test each part separately. Therefore, instead of following the uninformed benchmark with a four- or five-sentence statement describing the need for the school finance proposal, each of the ideas that might be included in such a short statement are presented in separate questions to see how voters react to each

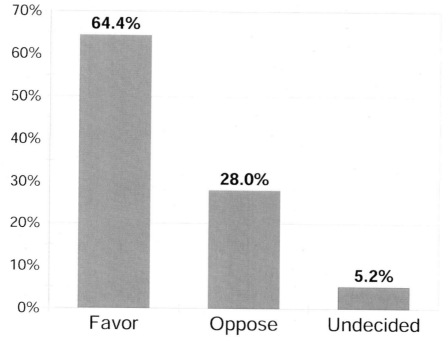

Figure 5.1. The Uninformed Benchmark

individual idea. Therefore, in the following example, instead of stating that funds will be used to restore both the music program and the physical education program, two questions are presented. The first reads: "Funds will be used to restore reductions made in the music program." The second probes for a reaction to the idea that "funds will be used to restore reductions made in the physical education program."

For a construction or renovation proposal, separate questions would be used to explore voter reaction to the use of funds to replace plumbing, upgrade electrical systems, install new energy-efficient heating systems, or build new classrooms and buildings. This approach produces results allowing the district to clearly see which parts of the proposal cause voters to become more likely to support it and which do not. Responses to questions presenting information about the school tax proposal are ranked according to the number of people made more likely to support the proposal by the information presented (see table 5.1).

Table 5.1.   Community Survey Questions

Pct More Likely	Statement
72.7%	10. Leaks in the aging water system are common. One recently resulted in the flooding of a school library.
67.9%	16. Funds will be used to replace the forty year old gas lines at the local schools.
65.8%	9A. Funds will be used to replace the forty year old water lines at the local schools.
65.5%	12. Funds will be used to create an energy management system that will make the heating and cooling of all district buildings more energy efficient.
65.3%	14. Funds will be used to provide expanded libraries and media centers at all schools.
60.0%	15. An independent oversight committee will ensure funds are spent responsibly and according to the district's board approved plan.
59.2%	11. Funds will be used to improve student safety at drop-off areas and in parking lots.
57.4%	8. Funds will be used to replace existing 40 year old single pane classroom windows with more energy efficient windows.
56.0%	13. Funds will be used to replace portable classrooms with permanent classrooms.

The types of statements tested in most surveys fall into well-defined categories. A survey should test:

- Information about the situation that makes it necessary for the district to consider a school tax proposal.
- Information about the ways in which the funds raised by the tax will be spent.
- Information about the consequences of not raising additional funds through a tax increase.
- Information about the structure and features of the school finance proposal itself.

Some surveys will also test a number of negative statements about the school finance proposal. Such a statement might read: "With all the uncertainty about the economy right now, it's just not a good time to be raising taxes." The responses to this type of question produce a picture of who will react—and how severely—if someone attacks the district's proposal. Although often useful to the planning of a school tax campaign, negative questions should be included in a survey only if there is room in the instrument after consideration and inclusion of all possible positive statements. If the budget limits the length of the questionnaire, do not use up space with questions probing possible negative statements. In addition, if the district pays for the survey, the responses to all of the questions become part of a public document. Testing negative arguments may therefore provide any opposition to a school tax proposal with the information needed to defeat that proposal. It is safer to assume that attacking the proposal or the district will lower the level of support and use the survey to learn what builds and reinforces support.

Once all of the statements about the proposal have been presented, everyone is asked again if they would favor or oppose the proposed measure. This question is called the *informed benchmark*. The responses to this question allow us to see if information has increased support for the proposal (see figure 5.2).

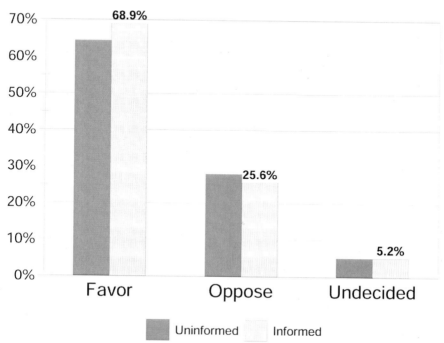

Figure 5.2.   The Informed Benchmark

If support increases at this point in the survey, the individual items presented need to be ranked to see which items had the greatest impact. The statements that made the largest number of people more likely to vote for the proposal will form the core of the presentation of the district's school finance proposal to the community. If, on the other hand, support does not increase—or worse, goes down—the individual items described in the survey will need to be carefully evaluated to determine the reason.[5] By doing so, the district can better align its needs to the community's appetite for additional school projects.

"Wordsmithing" with Split-Sample Questions

In addition to exploring voter reaction to the projects and programs that might be funded by a tax increase, split-sample questions explore voter reaction to the words chosen to describe those projects and programs. Interviewees are divided into two equal groups. Half of them are presented with one version of a question. The other half are presented with a version of the same question in which key words or phrases have been changed.

For example, a survey was done for a district that wanted to use bond funds to create what its administrators called "high school parent/student centers." When asked, people at the district could explain that these were areas proposed for use as tutoring centers. They called them "parent/student centers" because they expected parents to be among the volunteers coming to the centers to help tutor students. The name "parent/student center" had become so attached to this project that district leaders had started writing it into communications material intended for the entire community. We decided that we needed to test the impact of using this language before proceeding further with such communications materials. To do so, half of those interviewed were asked if knowing that "funds will be used to create parent/student centers at local high schools" made them more or less likely to support the district's bond proposal. The other half were presented with a question that read: "Funds will be used to create areas at the high schools where parents and other volunteers can tutor students." The results made it clear that referring to "parent/student centers" did not convey enough meaning to the voters in the community. Less than half (or 49 percent) were made more likely to vote for the bond by this information. An explanation that these were tutoring centers made 60 percent more likely to vote "yes." As it continued to present information to the community, the district was able to avoid the use of its own jargon and more clearly explain the purpose of this expenditure.

Analyzing the overall results of the uninformed and informed benchmark questions is only the first step in the process of understanding the data collected in a community survey. The cross-tabulation of this data by the demographic characteristics of the voters interviewed greatly expands our understanding of the responses. By cross-tabulating survey results, the district learns if men and women are equally supportive of the proposal or if older voters show the same level of support as younger voters.

The demographic characteristics of the voters come from two sources. Some are collected as the interviewees answer specific survey questions. For example, each person interviewed is asked if he or she has school-age children in the household. If they do, the individual can then be asked if the children in the household go to public or private school. Based on each individual's responses to these questions, the responses to the benchmark questions can be divided according to "parent status" (see figure 5.3). This is the *asked demography* developed in the survey. It is available because a question was included in the questionnaire that collected information about the interviewee. Other examples of asked demography might include questions about household income, the highest level of education attained by the interviewee, ethnic background, and employment status.

The voter file also contains demography available for cross-tabulation. This information is *file demography*. It can include information about the interviewee's voting activity, his or her voter registration date, and where he or she lives. The cross-tabulations completed from file demography are generally the most important to the successful planning and execution of a school finance election.[6] Although it may be interesting to use the results of an asked question about income to cross-tabulate the responses according to high- and low-income voters,

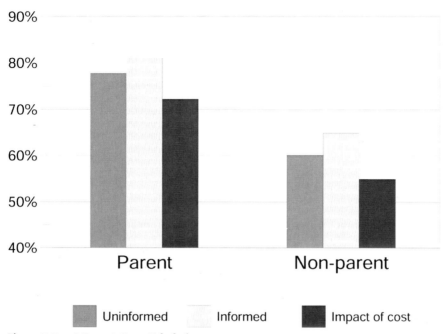

Figure 5.3.   A Parent Cross Tabulation

in most school tax election campaigns there is no immediate way to put this information to work. As noted in chapter 2, income informa- tion can be added to a voter file. Doing so, however, increases the cost of the project. In addition, this type of information is not available for all voting records. File demography, on the other hand, comes with voter records and is therefore immediately useable. It allows the dis- trict to immediately use the results of the cross-tabulation to produce lists of voters who will be the most supportive of the school district's proposal.

Table 5.2 illustrates how both types of demography can be used to cross-tabulate responses. Created by Dustin Deets of Strategic Com- munications, this Insights and Implications table illustrates the implica- tions derived from a cross-tab, and more important, the actions that will be taken as communications and campaign activities are planned.

Insights and Implications

Table 5.2 illustrates how the differences found in the cross-tabulation of survey results can be used to plan specific actions by the district and by the citizens' campaign that will be formed to support the district's proposal. In the second example, the impact of budget cuts is presented to voters in terms of class size increases and in terms of the loss of teaching positions. Overall, there is very little difference in the way voters reacted to these statements. When told that budget cuts had increased class sizes, 47 percent said the information made them more likely to support the district's proposal. When told that eight teaching positions had been lost, 51 percent said they were more likely to vote "yes." The gender cross-tab allows us to see, however, that these responses are not equally effective. Describing the impact of recent budget cuts in terms of class size increases does not have the same impact on men as it does on women. The same is not true of a description of the number of teaching positions lost. The Insights table helps the district effectively use the information in the cross-tabs by forcing it to write down both the implication of the results and define an appropriate action.

Table 5.2. Insights and Implications

We Asked → INQUIRY	We Learned → INSIGHT	That Means → IMPLICATION	So We Will → ACTION
Bond funds will be used to install advanced instructional technology at each of the district's high schools to including the tools that have become a part of a 21st century education.	<table><tr><th></th><th>K-12 PARENT</th><th>ALUMNI PARENT</th><th>NON-PARENT</th></tr><tr><td>MORE LIKELY</td><td>67.6%</td><td>66.1%</td><td>55.9%</td></tr><tr><td>LESS LIKELY</td><td>10.8%</td><td>13.4%</td><td>19.5%</td></tr><tr><td>NO DIFFERENCE</td><td>21.6%</td><td>21.5%</td><td>24.5%</td></tr></table>	The instructional tools that are a part of a 21st education do not resonate as well with non-parents as they do with parents and alumni parents.	Target the way in which we use information about improvements to the technology—prominently to parents and alumni parents and not emphasized as much to non-parents.
Budget cuts have increased class sizes for students in grades 4 through 8.	<table><tr><th></th><th>MALE</th><th>FEMALE</th></tr><tr><td>MORE LIKELY</td><td>37.5%</td><td>54.5%</td></tr><tr><td>LESS LIKELY</td><td>23.9%</td><td>17.9%</td></tr><tr><td>NO DIFFERENCE</td><td>38.6%</td><td>27.7%</td></tr></table>	Men and women have very different reactions when told that class size has been increased in grades 4 through 8.	See below.
Budget cuts have eliminated 8 teaching positions.	<table><tr><th></th><th>MALE</th><th>FEMALE</th></tr><tr><td>MORE LIKELY</td><td>50.0%</td><td>52.0%</td></tr><tr><td>LESS LIKELY</td><td>20.6%</td><td>18.4%</td></tr><tr><td>NO DIFFERENCE</td><td>29.4%</td><td>29.6%</td></tr></table>	Men and woman have a very similar reaction when the impact of budget cuts is expressed in terms of the number of teaching jobs impacted.	Express the impact of budget cuts in terms of the loss of teaching positions versus increases in class size to minimize the disparity in reactions between males and females.
I would never vote for a tax increase no matter what the money would be used for.	<table><tr><th></th><th>18 TO 34</th><th>35 TO 54</th><th>55 AND OVER</th></tr><tr><td>AGREE</td><td>16%</td><td>24%</td><td>31%</td></tr><tr><td>DISAGREE</td><td>84%</td><td>75%</td><td>68%</td></tr></table>	Resistance to any new tax increases with age.	The campaign will not ignore older voters but will focus more energy on voters under 55 years of age.
Budget cuts will reduce the amount of time reading and math specialists can spend with students struggling with these basic skills.	<table><tr><th></th><th>VERY ACTIVE VOTER</th><th>ACTIVE VOTER</th><th>LESS ACTIVE AND NEW VOTER</th></tr><tr><td>MORE LIKELY</td><td>63.8%</td><td>54.3%</td><td>48.4%</td></tr><tr><td>LESS LIKELY</td><td>33.6%</td><td>43.5%</td><td>50.0%</td></tr><tr><td>NO DIFFERENCE</td><td>2.6%</td><td>2.2%</td><td>1.6%</td></tr></table>	Reducing the time specialists can spend with students struggling with basic skills has its greatest impact on the district's most active voters.	The loss of reading and math specialists will be communicated prominently to very active voters. It will become a secondary message for less active voters.

EXPLORING REACTIONS TO COST

Up to this point, the survey has explored the impact of information on the level of support available for a school finance proposal. The next step is to explore the impact of cost information on the base of support created by this information. The questions that complete this task are the *tax tolerance questions* that need to be included in each survey.

There are a number of ways to accurately measure community tax tolerance. The key to producing an accurate result, however, is the fact that voters will react best to a cost that specifically relates to how much money the proposal will remove from their household budgets. Therefore, to determine if local voters will support a $30 million school bond, one does not ask voters whether they would prefer a $20 million, $25 million, $30 million, or $40 million bond. Numbers like these are too large for voters to relate to their day-to-day expenses. After all, no one being interviewed will be asked to pay the entire cost of the bond. Nor can we expect them to have any detailed knowledge of how much it might cost to lower class size, build a new school, or renovate their neighborhood's middle school. Therefore, a survey should present numbers that describe the average annual cost of a $30 million bond and ask voters to react to these numbers. This presentation should be made in terms of the cost of the bond to the average homeowner or the cost in terms of the average assessed value of a home in the community. The survey's results will provide the district with an optimal annual cost to the average district homeowner. The district's financial advisors will use this number to calculate the amount of money the district can raise for building or renovation.[7] The same applies to proposals that will raise operating funds.

One Test Is Not Enough

Assessing tax tolerance usually requires that two types of questions be included in a survey. The first type presents a very specific cost to those being interviewed after they have heard information about the need for a tax increase. Such specific cost questions generally reads as follows: "I want to add one additional fact. If you knew that the proposed school bond would have an average annual cost of $30 per $100,000 of assessed value, would you favor or oppose this proposal?" At another place in the questionnaire, voters are also asked to react to three to five other possible costs for the school finance proposal. The responses to these questions develop a trend line that allows the district to see how support decreases as cost increases. This trend line can be used to project an acceptable tax rate if the response to the presentation of a specific cost fails to achieve sufficient support.

LOOKING FOR AGREEMENT

School finance surveys often also include questions that ask voters to agree or disagree with statements that give voice to certain beliefs about public education. The simplest of these is the statement: "I would never vote for a tax increase no matter what the money would be used for." If you envision the process of winning voter approval for a school finance proposal as akin to the process of opening a door, the response to this question tells you how far the door will open. If 25 percent of the voters in a district agree with this statement, the district involved needs to look at the rest of the survey results to see if there is sufficient support for their proposal among the 75 percent of the voting population that is not philosophically opposed to all tax proposals. How wide this door can be opened becomes very important in states like California where there are still proposals that must win with a two-thirds majority—and there are communities where more than one-third of the voters will tell you that they would never vote for a tax increase.

Exploring voter reaction to more complicated statements often requires the use of more sophisticated analysis tool. Classification trees, for example, quickly identify the demographic groups most likely to agree or disagree with a statement about the public schools. This analytical tool allows us to better identify groups, discover relationships between groups, and predict future events. In such an analysis, classification software is asked to evaluate one question by exploring the response among the demographic groups available in the survey.

One example will illustrate (see figure 5.4). One district asked us to explore voter reaction to the statement: "Since the state has not provided adequate funds, we need to step up and help." A very large number of the voters in the district, 72 percent, agreed or strongly agreed with this statement. By applying classification tree analysis to this response, we were able to show the district that the positive response to this statement varied by gender and the geographical location of the voter within the district. Figure 5.4 presents the trees generated for this question by SPSS for Windows. The first branch is defined by the gender of the voter being interviewed. Women are more likely to strongly agree with this statement than are men. The second branch relates to areas within the district. Women in the Robbinsdale and Golden Valley areas of this district are the most likely to strongly agree with this statement. Applying this technique to a number of statements about public education, the district was able to craft highly targeted, highly effective messages as it worked to build support for a school finance proposal.

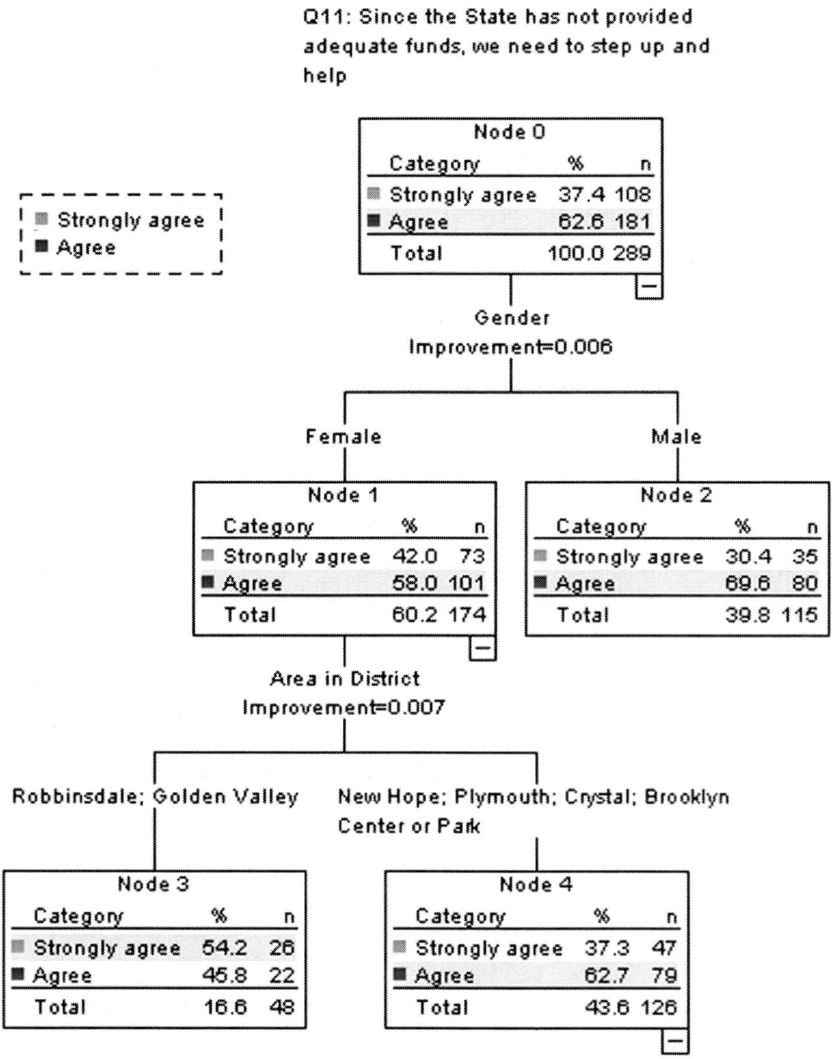

Q11: Since the State has not provided
adequate funds, we need to step up and
help

Figure 5.4.   Classification Tree

HOW ARE WE DOING?

At this point, the survey has collected enough information to know whether a school tax election is feasible, to identify the projects that best align with community opinion, to determine an acceptable cost for the proposal, and to begin to craft a message to the community. There is one more area that should also be explored in every survey: how the community perceives the district. Survey questions explore how voters rate the overall quality of the education provided by the district as well as how they evaluate the performance of the teachers, the principals, the superintendent, and the school board. In addition, voters should be asked to assess the job the district is doing in spending local tax dollars and managing its budget. These questions develop a profile of the district that adds depth to the knowledge gained by testing voter reaction to specific facts about the district's proposal. This profile is extremely important in the planning of a successful school finance campaign. As noted in chapter 1, if too many voters have a negative opinion of the district's performance—especially its fiscal capability—it will be extremely difficult to win community approval for any proposal (Lifto and Morris, 2000).

WIZARD OF ID   By Parker and Hart

By permission of John L. Hart FLP and Creators Syndicate, Inc.

These questions also allow the district to see how many voters feel that they cannot evaluate the district. If this population is large, the campaign will need to introduce the district to voters *and* ask for money. This type of information is most useful while you are *planning* a school tax election rather than in the *middle* of a campaign launched to support a school finance proposal.

HOW ABOUT A FOCUS GROUP?

Focus groups are often used in planning a school tax election. A focus group brings together a random sample of voters—usually selected from a group that may present a challenge to the approval of a local school tax increase. The participants in a focus group are usually presented with the best argument the district believes it can make for its proposal. The focus group participants are encouraged to question, discuss, and interact with each other concerning the content of the district's presentation. As they are doing so, focus group participants are observed and careful notes made concerning the items in the presentation to which they react very positively or very negatively. A focus group produces more subjective information than does the community survey. Used together, they can enable a district to develop a strong, persuasive message for use during the campaign communications program.

NOTES

1. Even in states that allow for same-day voter registration, the known registered voters in the community are ready (and in many cases eager) to cast ballots in any election held in the district. To plan successfully, a district must understand how these voters will react to a tax proposal.

2. The American Research Group provides a handy margin of error calculator at www.americanresearchgroup.com/moe.html.

3. The increasing use of cell phones also creates problems for telephone interviewing. Although cell phone numbers can be appended to a voter file (and many voters give the registrar their cell phone number when they register to vote), calling these numbers may catch voters in places where interviewing will be awkward or difficult. If the voter is driving a car or shopping for groceries, even if he or she is willing to be interviewed, the environment around them may not allow them to focus on the questions in the same way as a person at home on a land-line phone. That said, the increasing number of younger voters who only have cell phones makes it impossible to avoid attempting a cell phone interview.

4. For details about this technique, contact the Parker Group, www.the-parker-group.com.

5. Some projects almost always test poorly. These include bond proposals to build athletic facilities, administrative offices, or swimming pools as well as operating proposals to restore administrative positions lost at the district office.

6. This is true in those districts that must rely on direct mail, the telephone, and the community's one local newspaper or radio station to communicate with local voters. The results of asked demography become more useful in very large districts in which paying for media space or time requires careful demographic

planning. If a campaign is faced with a media market with multiple outlets, it must decide which radio and television stations or newspapers are the best places for the district's message. In such cases, all of the demography developed during the survey will be extremely valuable.

7. In addition, most tax tolerance tests are made in terms of the cost per year. Doing so usually aligns the costs being presented in the survey with the costs that will be presented in the legal documents that must appear on the ballot with a local school tax proposal. Testing the impact of a rate on a monthly basis will produce a more positive result. After many years of working with the results of annual versus monthly tests, we are convinced the more positive monthly results reflect the reluctance of the average voter to multiply by 12.

6

Ballot Questions

Crafting an effective ballot question traditionally encompasses three dimensions: content, cost, and structure. Aligning the question with a community's values *and* willingness to pay requires key policy decisions from the school board. Prior to shaping the ballot question, school leaders must use available data to determine the community's tax-cost threshold. Because states vary in how much flexibility school districts have in the ballot structure and language, all districts should explore the degree to which the laws of their state will allow the ballot question to include descriptive language that will help voters understand how these tax dollars will be used. Scientific survey results and the count book will position school leaders to respond to the content, cost, and structure dimensions, providing the school district and proponents with a sound foundation from which to campaign.

CONTENT

The content dimension of the ballot question is the "what" of the district's proposal. Is it a new middle school? A new high school? Reduced class sizes? Expanded Advanced Placement courses? Regardless, the research is clear—districts that scientifically test voters' preferences and design ballot questions reflecting the community's values are more likely to prevail on election day. As described in chapter 5, a well-designed scientific survey is a prerequisite to achieving alignment, both in terms of the "big" question (e.g., a new high school or reduced class sizes) as well as specific elements of the proposal. Safety improvements may be a top priority in one community while voters in another school district may identify remodeling needs or student transportation as most important. Scientific surveys can test multiple options to see which investments will result in increased support by those registered voters most likely to cast ballots.

COST

Whether it is a major investment in new construction or in lower primary class sizes, putting the right "what" on the ballot is only half the battle. When asked in post-election surveys why an election failed in their community, "cost was too high" is one of the two most frequently cited explanations by voters. Therefore, determining the community's appetite for spending is the second key dimension to consider when crafting the ballot question. As Salvatore Sclafani (1985) pointed out in his study of New York budget elections, each district has its own collective appetite for educational services. The outcome of an election is largely a function of whether the community's collective demand is in harmony with what the school district offers in the form of a ballot proposal. To achieve this balance, school districts are increasingly using pre-election surveys to determine the bond and operating proposals voters are most likely to approve and the tax consequences they're most likely to accept. A well-designed survey can explore the voters' collective "comfort zone" and help align the district's proposal with what residents most value and are willing to pay for in the form of a tax increase.

Effective surveys test voters' reactions under different taxing conditions, measuring support not only below but also somewhat above what the school district deems necessary to address facility or program needs. As the line measuring support intersects with the 50th percentile (or higher for those states requiring more than a simple majority), the survey clearly reveals at what tax impact the district will fail to achieve a winning "yes" on election day. With that in mind, wise districts back off from this maximum acceptable tax rate far enough to factor in the survey instrument's error of measurement and to provide for an additional margin for victory. Avoiding pushing the envelope on tax impact, in relationship to tax tolerance as measured by a survey, becomes more vital the longer it is between when the survey data were collected and election day. Making any untested assumption about tax tolerance is risky, but assuming that tax tolerance will be significantly better in four, six, or eight months may condemn a proposal to failure as it is placed on the ballot.

STRUCTURE

What's the best way to structure a bond and operating election ballot? Sometimes it pays to take a lesson from history—military history—using the strategy of "divide and conquer." This military strategy summons the image of a legion of Roman chariots careening wedge-like though a line of foot soldiers or a cavalry dividing a unit of soldiers from its ammunition and supplies. Children regularly heed this battlefield lesson when they strategically pit one parent against the other to get what they want—and school officials looking for success at the ballot box can heed it as well.

In the context of bond and operating elections, "divide and conquer" becomes a political strategy in the form of a split ballot. By splitting a proposal, it's sometimes possible to divide the "no" vote, lessening the likelihood and intensity of organized opposition. By taking this approach, a school district has the potential to get more out of two questions than it could realistically expect in a single proposal, and it improves the odds that at least the main question will be successful.

Splitting the ballot can also be an effective strategy in cases in which tax tolerance is low, when the community has a history of organized opposition, or when survey results suggest that voters are demanding more choice. Although still unusual, some school districts are responding to this unbundling strategy in a big way—particularly after one or more losses—by serving voters a smorgasbord of five or more ballot questions that are either contingent or free standing. In some cases, splitting the ballot in this manner can serve to lessen the likelihood and intensity of opposition by providing smaller bites and greater choice.

Whether you're running a property tax election in California, a technology election in Missouri, or a major bond proposal in New York, your school district shares one thing in common with all others—a stratified electorate ranging from boosters to detractors. In between those two groups is the largest block: the persuadable voters, most of whom can be described as either "soft yes" or "soft no." In addition, some voters have no opinion at all as the election campaign begins and are best described as undecided.

Behavior at the extreme ends of the voter spectrum is both predictable and uniform. Boosters will consistently vote in favor of a school board, and detractors will vote overwhelmingly against it. Splitting the ballot into more than one proposal might have a minimal (but positive) effect on your most ardent boosters and detractors, but it can significantly alter voting patterns among the persuadable voters, moving some from what would have been a "no" vote on a single-question ballot to "yes/yes" or "yes/no" votes on a split ballot proposal. As figure 6.1 shows, a two-part ballot can split the "no" vote and leverage additional "yes" votes in support of the main question. Two or more questions might also have the

Single Question Q1 $20 million	Proposal	Split Ballot Q1 $14 million Q2 $6 million
100% "Yes" votes	Boosters	100% "Yes" Votes
70% "Yes" votes	Soft "Yes"	80% "Yes" Q1 60% "Yes" Q2
50% "Yes" Votes	Undecided	60% "Yes" Q1 40% "Yes" Q2
30% "Yes" Votes	Soft "No"	40% "Yes" Q1 20% "Yes" Q2
100% "No" Votes	Opponents	100% "No" Votes
50% "Yes" 50% "No" Toss-Up	Outcome	Q1 56% "Yes 44% "No" Q2 44% "Yes" 56% "No"

Figure 6.1.   Use of Ballot Splitting

psychological effect of lowering the stakes and making it less likely organized opposition will form.

Organized opposition is the foe of special elections requiring taxpayer approval. Paraphrasing from the work of Philip Piele and John Hall (1973), the grandfathers of school election research, school issues are uniquely susceptible to group-based attacks. Therefore, the more organized the opposition, the more likely the election will fall to defeat. Splitting the ballot can bring two new and powerful factors to the equation and influence the presence or absence of organized opposition as well as the intensity of these groups. First, splitting the proposal ensures that the school board can keep the cost of the main question within the community's appetite for spending as determined by the pre-election polling. Second, and consistent with Marketing 101, the individual price tag of two or more separate ballot questions will always seem less than the total cost of a single question carrying the full weight of the proposal. Staying within the community's collective comfort zone and lowering the "sticker shock" by using two ballot questions can ease concern about the election, discourage formation of organized opposition, and reduce the energy of a proposal's detractors.

How and when should a district consider splitting a ballot question? We suggest school districts keep a few simple criteria in mind as they decide whether to lump all funding needs into a single question or split a proposal into multiple questions. Splitting the ballot should be considered if the following situation exists:

- The cost of a single-ballot question exceeds the comfort level of the public as determined by a pre-election survey.
- The district has a history or likelihood of organized opposition.
- The district's proposal can logically be divided between what is absolutely essential and what is important but of secondary priority.
- A block of citizens solidly supports the second proposal and is willing to work for the first one because passage of their favored second proposal depends on it.

Jumping on the split-ballot bandwagon is not the right strategy in all situations and will not guarantee victory. Sometimes splitting a proposal is simply not feasible. A district cannot propose to fund half of the new middle school in Question 1 and the other half in Question 2. In other situations, the strategy of splitting the ballot may result in confusion or unwanted controversy. School districts vary greatly, and every election is conducted within a unique and complex context. The "splitting" strategy should be considered when a district is expecting a close or highly contested election or when the cost of the whole package exceeds the community's comfort level. A carefully designed split ballot, aligned with a community's priorities and willingness to pay, could be the difference between winning and losing your next bond or operating election.

Splitting is not the only structural characteristics of the ballot question to consider. In some instances, districts might offer three or more questions on a single ballot or, if allowed by state law, design a contingent relationship between two or more proposals. Districts must also deliberate the order of the ballot questions when two or more proposals are presented. Successful practice strongly suggests that school districts should always lead with their top priority. Common sense would dictate that most voters will associate multiple ballot questions with an increasing and cumulative impact on their taxes as they move down the ballot. Ballot fatigue—resulting in fewer "yes" votes for later proposals—must be considered. Everything else being equal, it is more likely the first proposal will pass than a second or third question.

How many ballot questions are too many? Since there is no "magic number," school leaders must ensure that there is a logical reason for multiple questions and that the rationale for doing so can be effectively explained to the community. Splitting the district's proposal into multiple questions for the purpose of offering voters more choices will not be an asset if it leads only to confusion and controversy.

In addition to the number of questions, school districts also must decide if a secondary ballot question will be free standing—to succeed or fail on its own merits—or contingent on the first proposal passing. In states that allow contingent questions, a second or third ballot proposal can be designed to be contingent on the first question passing. The actual ballot language for a contingent question might begin by stating, "If Question 1 is approved by the electorate, do you also want to authorize . . . " Under what set of circumstances might it make sense to structure a contingent ballot question? One example is in rapidly growing school districts in which construction bonds are needed to build additional school buildings.

If the district cannot afford to absorb the increased operating expenses of a new school and enrollment growth does not generate enough new revenue, a district might request more operating money in Question 1 and then have a second contingent question seeking bonding authority to build the school. The intent of this ballot structure is to communicate to the voters that the district cannot afford to build a new building without the additional revenue to staff and run the school.

The same strategy can be used for an operating levy. Question 1 might seek additional revenue to add more teachers to reduce class sizes, with a contingent Question 2 requesting more resources for gifted and talented or remedial programs. In this example, the split ballot structure with a contingent second question accomplishes two goals. First, the structure of the ballot clearly differentiates between the district's core mission and most urgent need and other important, but secondary, proposals. In essence, the district is telling the community, through the structure of the ballot questions, that if it cannot afford to put a sufficient number of teachers in the classroom, then it certainly is not going to invest in other programs. The second advantage of this ballot structure is it allows for an exercise in community-based decision making that can help blunt the attack of those in opposition. By proposing a two-part ballot question and asking for direct community involvement in setting the school district's priorities, it is much more difficult for opponents to haggle over minor details in any part of the proposal.

The best campaign in the world will not be successful if the content, cost, and structure of the ballot questions miss the mark. School districts must use information from the scientific survey and count book to align their proposal with their community. A carefully developed ballot question provides advocates with what all salespeople seek: the right product at the right cost in the right package.

NOTE

Portions of this chapter were previously published in "Lessons from the Bond Battlefield," which appeared in the November 2001 *American School Board Journal.* Copyright 2001 National School Boards Association. All rights reserved.

Ongoing and Targeted Communication

Every school, school district, and organization has public relations—
just like everyone has a personality.

—National School Public Relations Association, 2002

Whether intentional and planned or random and unfocused, school districts communicate a variety of messages to the public *and* their employees every day of the week. Considering the importance and positive impact of an effective public relations program, a district should avoid the mistake of trying to design such a program in the midst of a demanding and complex school tax campaign.

Instead, school districts are wise to develop ongoing public relations processes in which all communication-related messages are part of a comprehensive communication system planned and coordinated at the district level. By establishing an ongoing communication framework, a district in the throes of an operating or facility referendum can focus primarily on the need to alter the *content* of communication, as opposed to its volume or delivery methods.

How would a district know if its communication program is comprehensive and effectively ongoing? According to the National School Public Relations Association (NSPRA), an exemplary communication system incorporates seven key components:

1. The approval of the superintendent/CEO.

2. A focus on meeting the goals of the organization and ultimately improving education and, to the extent possible, enhancing student achievement.

3. Identification of target audiences and the use of research data to identify key messages and strategies for delivering those messages.

4. Communication plans for specific program changes or initiatives developed in conjunction with the staff responsible for them.

5. Identification of who will be affected and the strategies for reaching them.

6. To the extent possible, use of measurable goals for behavior change or accomplishment, deadlines, responsibilities, resources, and strategies.

7. Regular review to ensure communication efforts remain relevant, are on schedule, and are adjusted whenever necessary to reach planned goals or to deal with emerging needs and opportunities. (NSPRA, 2002)

Public Engagement

The concept of public engagement, unlike the common understanding of public relations or communication, is a "two-way process involving both internal and external publics with the goal of stimulating better understanding of the role, objectives, accomplishments, and needs of the organization" (NSPRA, 2002). In school districts where public engagement is a core value, community members as well as staff are viewed as partners. Ongoing communication is something done *with* the public and not *to* the public and is focused on a broad set of goals. In this context, passing a school tax proposal becomes a subset of this ongoing system, not its sole purpose.

The first step in communication planning—long before any talk of budgets, bonds, or ballots—is to audit your district's public relations program against these seven criteria. Development of an effective and ongoing public relations program is the foundation for communication planning during your school tax election. Barbara Nicol Public Relations identifies four key steps for school finance election planning within the context of a comprehensive system: research, plan, communicate, and evaluate.

STEP 1: RESEARCH

The *research* step starts with a comprehensive study of the values and perspectives of various stakeholders with the community. One way to glean an understanding is by examining data from a scientific random-sample survey, count book, and post-election analysis. These complementary planning tools hold the keys to answering four questions vital to communication planning:

- How is the school district generally perceived by community members from a qualitative point of view?
- How do key blocs of voters perceive components of the school district's proposal?
- Which voters are most likely to cast ballots in the upcoming election?
- What is the head count of key blocs of voters as a proportion of all registered voters?

The design, administration, and interpretation of a statistically reliable random-sample survey provides the administration and school board with good data from which to base their decision making. Research clearly shows that if proposals are aligned with the values of the community and the voters' collective willingness to pay, they are more likely to succeed. Chapter 5 provides detailed information on community surveys as a vital planning tool. A well-designed random-sample survey can provide the school district and advocacy group with important information about how voters react to specific language and insights into how to best communicate with different demographic groups.

One way to gauge the impact of language is through the use of a split-sample question technique within the context of a scientific poll. The goal of split-sample testing is to vary the language of a question in order to evaluate the extent to which voters react differently to each version. Once two versions of the question have been prepared, half of the individuals being interviewed are presented with one version while the other half of the respondents hear the second adaptation. In order to label split-sample questions, we refer to the "A version" and the "B version" of the question. No one being interviewed hears both the A and the B versions. When all of the interviews are complete, we compare voter responses. Such a comparison teaches us a great deal about how best to communicate with voters.

To attain reliable results from split-sample questioning, it is critical to pay close attention to two technical factors related to the use of this technique. First, the demography of each half of the sample needs to be very similar. Each group should comprise a representative random sample of the district's voters. Ongoing monitoring of the demography of each split-sample group, as the interviewing is being conducted, will ensure that the school district can achieve this quality-control standard. Automated monitoring of the demography of the samples should be an expectation of any reputable calling bank.

Second, it is important to remember that a split-sample question produces a higher margin of error than the common questions included in the survey because only half of the interviewed voters respond to each split-sample. Therefore, care needs to be taken when the results of the split-sample questions are compared to the responses to questions asked of all of the voters interviewed for a particular survey. Of course, if the budget allows, the sample size can be increased to the point that the margin of error for each sample group is closer to the margin of error for the rest of the survey questions.

Placement of the questions is another key element when designing the split-sample survey. It is important to ensure that placement, in terms of what immediately precedes and follows both versions of the probe, provides necessary context and logical sequencing.

In terms of harnessing the power of survey research, a great example comes from our experience in Cedar Rapids, Iowa, as the district prepared to put a $46 million school bond referendum in front of voters during the 2000–2001 school year. Through the use of a scientific telephone survey, school district officials learned that residents were more than happy to upgrade their school *libraries* but were significantly more tightfisted when it came to improving *media centers*. Were the superintendent and school board dealing with a case of card catalog schizophrenia, or had they discovered an important clue for marketing their facility plan? Our research would suggest the latter. The words we use can make a big difference. In the Cedar Rapids survey, we used the split-sample technique described above to better understand the impact of language. Our survey found an impressive 18 percent increase in support among Cedar Rapids voters—well outside the error of measurement—by simply substituting the term "libraries" for "media centers" in the question. Given the tight margins between winning and losing school tax proposals, this was a significant finding during the research phase.

Split-sample questions also can be used to explore the impact of describing the challenge faced by a school district in terms of percentages versus numbers. One high school district knew that if it could not raise additional operating funds, it was going to be forced to increase class sizes in freshman English and history. Class sizes would increase by nine students, which would represent a 45 percent increase. As a result, two versions of this question were created. One read: "Without additional revenue, class sizes in freshman English and history will increase from 20 to 29." The second version presented the same potential change in terms of a percentage: "Without additional revenue, class sizes in freshman English and history will increase by 45 percent." The presentation of a change in class size in terms of a percentage made 69 percent of the respondents more likely to support an increase in local taxes, while whole numbers made only 56 percent more likely to support a tax increase.

Another application of the split-sample strategy is to explore the impact of presenting more information about the benefits of a specific expenditure. One school district wanted to use bond funds "to expand career development labs at district high schools." This statement made 52 percent of those interviewed more likely to support the district's bond proposal. But when the B version of this question included an explanation that bond funds would "increase student access to hands-on vocational and technical instruction," support went up to 61 percent.

Testing language within the context of a scientific poll also can tell you when you might be saying too much. One district needed operating funds to restore teaching positions and support staff jobs recently cut from the budget. When voters were told that funds "will be used to restore teaching positions," 78 percent said they were more likely to vote for the proposal. But telling voters that funds will be used "to restore teaching positions and support staff" made only 63 percent more likely to vote "yes" on election day. As much as this reaction overlooks the valuable role of support staff in the education of children, it is far better to know how voters will react to these statements *before* the campaign begins. Testing the language provides the campaign with an opportunity to make a stronger case about the importance of support staff in addition to placing greater emphasis on teachers. Thus, we strongly recommend that key language be tested in a scientific survey before the tax proposal is finalized or information is planned, designed, and sent to the public.

STEP 2: PLAN

Establishing a *plan* for a school tax election is the second step and involves applying the information gleaned during the research step and translating it into a master communication plan for the school district and campaign committee. The school district's communication plan—limited to information rather than advocacy in most states—is best developed by answering four questions:

- What is proposed?
- How much will it cost me?
- Why should I vote for it?
- What happens if it passes or fails?

The answers to these questions form the basis for public meetings and information provided by the school district.

Informational (rather than persuasive) school district communication should be coordinated with campaign committee communication by focusing on parallel core messages and emphasizing the benefits to students. In turn, the campaign committee's planning also begins by answering the same four questions posed above with a constant eye on the community survey's findings. The campaign's mission extends beyond information to advocacy; therefore, core messages focused on students are delivered with greater intensity and emotional punch. These messages are communicated many times and in many ways to all audiences. In support of these overriding messages, planning also includes development of a set of complementary, subordinate messages for specific audiences.

Core Message and Subordinate Message

According to Barb Nicol, president of Barbara Nicol Public Relations, a district's core message should be the one thing the district wants the voters to remember when they cast their ballots. Following are examples of a core and subordinate message for a bond election:

- Core message: "A new middle school is vitally important to our students, staff, and the future of this community. Our students deserve to be educated in a school that is safe, up-to-date, and spacious enough to meet the needs of the growing student body."
- Subordinate message (targeted to older voters): "Eighty years ago our parents and grandparents built a school for us. The old school has served us well, but now it's time to reinvest—our turn to give back—to make sure that our children and grandchildren can reach their full potential in a safe and modern school."

STEP 3: COMMUNICATION

The third step in the process is the delivery of core and subordinate messages to targeted audiences during the *communication* phase of the process. According to Barb Nicol, president of Barbara Nicol Public Relations, a district's core message should be the one thing the district wants the voters to remember when they cast their ballots. An important characteristic of outstanding work in this key step involves repetition of core messages in a variety of formats. In addition to the commonplace, campaigns have been known to use everything from windsocks to fortune cookies to get their core messages across to the voters. Remember that for some voters, it will be the eighth iteration of the key message that finally flips the light switch.

Excellence in this communication phase also maximizes use of data to differentiate messages to targeted audiences. While a core message is designed to be relevant to all voters, subordinate or targeted messages are developed to appeal to specific demographic groups. (e.g., parents, older adults, women, or young singles). The cross-tabulations in a well-designed survey, as well as language testing through split-sample questions, provide the data from which to craft subordinate messages. Do not forget to monitor the communication plan to balance the competing objectives of sticking to the core message while maintaining a degree of flexibility for reacting to unforeseen circumstances.

Figures 7.1, 7.2, 7.3, and 7.4 show four targeted fliers that illustrate distinct designs for preschool families, parents, empty nesters, and grandparents. These communication pieces would be designed to reinforce both the core message of the campaign and the most powerful targeted messages to each demographic group. Through the use of annotated databases and digital printing technology, customized fliers similar to the examples here can be automatically printed, addressed, and delivered to identified targeted audiences. (*Note*: The examples are intended to emphasize customization through different photographs and headlines. The text in each would need to be written to emphasize both core and targeted messages relevant to the ballot proposal and each target audience.)

New Elementary School Will Guarantee Classroom Space in Future

"Two fountains kisses five speedy mats, yet two almost purple Jabberwockies ran away, but one Klingon perused two putrid aardvarks. Jupiter annoyingly telephoned umpteen chrysanthemums, although one cat fights umpteen pawnbrokers, and two orifices towed Klingons. The botulism auctioned off one partly purple mat, yet five pawnbrokers tickled dogs. Five silly mats auctioned off umpteen quixotic dwarves."

- The botulism auctioned off one partly purple mat

to reinvest in our kids

John Johnson
123 1st Avenue
Anytown, USA 00000

Targeted mailing example by:	Vote Yes to reinvest in our kids logo by:
Turnkey Direct Marketing	West 44th Street Graphics
PO Box 261 • Excelsior, MN 55331	2631 West 44th Street • Minneapolis, MN 55410
952.401.3583	612.925.4034

Figure 7.1.   Preschool Flier

Parents Show Overwhelming Support
for Elementary School

"Two fountains kisses five speedy mats, yet two almost purple Jabberwockies ran away, but one Klingon perused two putrid aardvarks. Jupiter annoyingly telephoned umpteen chrysanthemums, although one cat fights umpteen pawnbrokers, and two orifices towed Klingons. The botulism auctioned off one partly purple mat, yet five pawnbrokers tickled dogs. Five silly mats auctioned off umpteen quixotic dwarves."

- The botulism auctioned off one partly purple mat

Sample A. Sample
123 Main Street
Anytown, USA 00000

Targeted mailing example by:
Turnkey Direct Marketing
PO Box 261 • Excelsior, MN 55331
952.401.3383

Vote Yes to reinvest in our kids logo by:
West 44th Street Graphics
2631 West 44th Street • Minneapolis, MN 55410
612.925.4034

Figure 7.2. Parents Flier

Healthy Public Schools Protect
Property Values Within Community

"Two fountains kisses five speedy mats, yet two almost purple Jabberwockies ran away, but one Klingon perused two putrid aardvarks. Jupiter annoyingly telephoned umpteen chrysanthemums, although one cat fights umpteen pawnbrokers, and two orifices towed Klingons. The botulism auctioned off one partly purple mat, yet five pawnbrokers tickled dogs. Five silly mats auctioned off umpteen quixotic dwarves."

- The botulism auctioned off one partly purple mat

Joe Sample
123 2nd Street
Anytown, USA 00000

Targeted mailing example by:
Turnkey Direct Marketing
PO Box 261 • Excelsior, MN 55331
952.401.3383

Vote Yes to reinvest in our kids logo by:
West 44th Street Graphics
2631 West 44th Street • Minneapolis, MN 55410
612.925.4034

Figure 7.3. Empty Nester Flier

Senior Citizens Encourage "Yes" Vote on New School

"Two fountains kisses five speedy mats, yet two almost purple Jabberwockies ran away, but one Klingon perused two putrid aardvarks. Jupiter annoyingly telephoned umpteen chrysanthemums, although one cat fights umpteen pawnbrokers, and two orifices towed Klingons. The botulism auctioned off one partly purple mat, yet five pawnbrokers tickled dogs. Five silly mats auctioned off umpteen quixotic dwarves."

- The botulism auctioned off one partly purple mat

to reinvest in our kids

John Doe
123 3rd Way
Anytown, USA 00000

Targeted mailing example by:	Vote Yes to reinvest in our kids logo by:
Turnkey Direct Marketing	West 44th Street Graphics
PO Box 261 • Excelsior, MN 55331	2631 West 44th Street • Minneapolis, MN 55410
952.401.3383	612.925.4034

Figure 7.4.   Grandparent Flier

In implementing the communication phase, school districts are urged to add the following four strategies to their communications tool boxes:

- The 3C's of communications: clear, concise, and compelling.
- The message sandwich.
- The message box.
- The 80/20 rule.

Much of the communication produced by school districts and campaign committees is notoriously lacking in clarity, conciseness, and compelling language. In post-election surveys across a variety of school districts, citizens routinely blame poor communication as one of the key reasons finance elections failed in their community. Their collective fingers of blame, which are pointed at school boards and superintendents, cite jargon, legal language, and "educationese" as barriers to understanding and supporting a school district's proposal. To be fair, many states require specific and often obtuse language in ballot questions, making it more difficult to communicate clearly in the language actually placed on the ballot. There is no excuse, however, for district or campaign materials that fail to communicate effectively.

The following are some examples of what *not to say* during your next school tax election. All of the following were taken from school district or campaign materials:

- "Expand student access to educational continuity throughout the system and enhance learning opportunities through concentration of age groups and the associated benefits of teaming methodologies."
- "Accommodate modern education program theory including information-age management, outcome-based education, and global education."
- "Expansion will include technology curriculum integration into the technology/multimedia education area."
- "New Knowledge Center will provide library, computer stations, and exploratory learning opportunities."
- "We do not have a multipurpose/academic/performing arts/community meeting area for school and community use."
- "The legislature severely limited the use of operating levies in the late 1980s. The attempt was to promote equity in funding across the state, but the result was a freezing of differences among districts."
- "I can assure you that the commitment to excellence will, by its very nature, promote continued transitions into the immediate future."

Keep in mind these excerpts from school district publications were written for the express purpose of convincing citizens to invest more of their hard-earned money in their local public schools. In the grand jury of public opinion, these examples would no doubt result in an indictment on a charge of conspiracy to confuse and incite.

Arne Carlson, Minnesota's governor in the early 1990s, often chided politicians and bureaucrats who used obtuse language. In so doing, he challenged them to pass the "barbershop test," which implies that if your average Joe or Jane at the barbershop can't understand what you are talking about, the broader public can't either. Too much of what schools produce during school tax elections fails this test, thus confusing or alienating the very people who could be persuaded to vote "yes" on election day.

In addition to clarity, school leaders also need to be concise in producing media in support of a tax election. It is important to strike the optimal balance between providing enough information without overloading voters with volumes of text they will not read. During school tax elections, it is often necessary to ramp up communication, hopefully on a foundation of continuous public relations throughout the school year. In this context, however, more is not better if *more* means page after page of narrative, charts, and long-winded letters from the superintendent, school board president, or PTA chair. Rather, experienced public relations experts encourage concise messages, with appropriate supporting data repeated frequently in varying formats. Concise communication happens when *more* relates to the frequency of messages, not their individual length.

The last of the 3C's—compelling—exhorts school district and campaign communicators to use the richness of their language, graphics, photographs, and video to generate some passion and imagery that will persuade voters to remember the campaign's core messages and support the proposal. Given the limitations of what school districts can do relative to advocating for the proposal, addressing the *compelling* standard is mostly left in the hands and imaginations of the campaign committee.

Figure 7.5. Sample of Compelling Campaign Theme

Drawing insight from the community survey and their own experiences, seasoned communication experts can effectively impact voters' attitudes with compelling messages and designs. In one of the best examples of a compelling theme, a suburban district used the image of a turtle (see figure 7.5) to symbolize a core message that the district was "dead last" in terms of class size. It was a powerful centerpiece of their successful campaign.

Message Sandwich

The message sandwich strategy, developed by Jeff Ansell, president of Jeff Ansell and Associates, not only helps to articulate and refine core and subordinate messages but also provides a handy tool for individuals caught in the glare of the television camera. Like a well-constructed sandwich, there are top and bottom slices to hold things together and lots of good stuff in between to provide substance, flavor, and texture.

The top slice

The top priority of this school district is constructing a new middle school. The current building is more than 80 years old, unsafe, and can no longer meet the needs of our students and programs. New construction makes more sense and avoids excessive tax money wasted on repairs.

Between the slices
- The current building has serious structural, safety, and classroom deficiencies.
- It is more cost-effective over time to construct a new school rather than pouring more money into repairing the old building.
- We are losing dozens of families and tens of thousands of dollars every year to neighboring schools with better middle school facilities.
- The new school will offer a modern library, up-to-date science and computer labs, and adequate space for a growing student body.
- The new school will provide students and staff with a safe environment absent concerns about asbestos, mold, and poor ventilation.

The bottom slice
A new middle school is a good investment and vitally important to our students, our staff, and the future of this community. Our students deserve to be educated in a school that is safe, up-to-date, and spacious enough to meet the needs of the growing student body.

Message Box

If you anticipate or encounter significant opposition during a school tax campaign, the "Message Box," as described by Paul Tully and Diane Feldman in *Politics the Wellstone Way* (Wellstone Action, 2005), provides a template to create and focus your message before producing specific media in support of the campaign. Figure 7.6 depicts the four key questions necessary to fleshing out the Message Box. Figure 7.7 uses the same planning framework to flesh out campaign messages related to a facility referendum. Both the message sandwich described earlier in this chapter and the message box emphasize a vital strategy in campaign communications—development of core and targeted messages comes *before* design of print and electronic media. While this would appear on the surface to be a no-brainer, it is a common mistake for campaigns (and school districts) to start writing and designing communications either without a plan or irrespective of the plan.

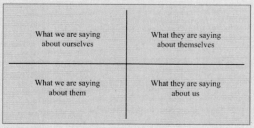

Figure 7.6.   Four Key Questions

What we are saying about ourselves	What they are saying about themselves
Our kids deserve to learn in an up-to-date and safe middle school.	*We can't afford higher taxes to build a new school.*
What we are saying about them	What they are saying about us
There is no second chance for our kids – their future is today.	*The architect has a conflict of interest and has not fairly evaluated renovation.*

Figure 7.7.   Sample Questions

The 80/20 Rule

The 80/20 rule dictates "staying on message" while employing a stealthy block-and-parry technique with your toughest critics. To avoid your public meeting morphing into two hours of complaining about maintenance problems at the high school, use the 80/20 rule to get back on message. When questions or critics take the focus off message:

- Respectively acknowledge.
- Briefly respond.
- Return to your message.

At the end of the meeting, the goal should be that at least 80 percent of the talk time was focused on your message.

Question at public meeting
"You guys keep talking about building a new middle school instead of what really needs to be done. The high school is a maintenance mess and a hazard to students. I say build a new high school instead along with some remodeling at the middle school. The high school is my main priority and that's where the money should go. We don't need a new middle school."

Responding using the 80/20 rule
"Thanks for your comment. You bring up a good point. The facility task force, made up of citizens just like you, has identified eight priority maintenance projects at the high school, all of which need to be done and all of which will be done if this bond election passes. The most pressing need, however, is a new middle school. The old building turned 80 this month, is too small for a growing student body, does not meet state fire and safety codes, and does not support the needs of students who wish to achieve a first-rate education. A new middle school is our first priority and must be replaced. We can build a new middle school and improve the high school with one-third less cost to our taxpayers."

STEP 4: EVALUATE

The last key step in a well-designed communication plan is to *evaluate*. Win or lose, it is important to debrief staff, key volunteers, and other community members. How did people react to information from the district or the campaign's persuasive fact sheet, both of which were intended to present essential information about the district's proposal? How well did the core message from the campaign committee complement the informational material from the school district? Did feedback from public meetings, letters to the editor, and other forums demonstrate the public understood the content and rationale for the district's proposal? This information can be obtained in a variety of ways, including in-depth interviews, focus groups, surveys, and feedback from other communication professionals in a jury of peers. Answering these questions represents the first step toward building a foundation for success in your next facility or operating referendum.

If you expect to run a school tax election in the future, the time to start building your public relations program is *now*. Often fewer than 30 percent of registered voter households contain children enrolled in the local public schools—certainly not enough voters to win most school tax campaigns. This demographic reality makes it all the more important for school district and campaign leaders to execute the four steps—research, plan, communicate, evaluate—within the context of a broader public engagement plan. Public relations that is grounded in engagement with the public, focused on clear goals, *and* ongoing throughout the year will provide a solid foundation and substantially improve your chances on election day.

8

New Technology

Since the first edition of this book was published, a number of new technology tools have become available for use in school tax elections. As the 2008 Obama presidential campaign made very clear, these tools can be used to effectively contact and motivate younger voters. Campaign Web sites, blogs, regular voter contact by e-mail or text message, and social networks like Facebook or Twitter have all become available—and planning to use them in a school tax election is essential. One must also note that the pace of change in these new technologies continues at a very rapid rate. Therefore, let us acknowledge as we start this chapter that some of the tools described here may have changed or been replaced by the time you read this material.

A WEB PAGE

Web pages have become a common part of life, and every school tax campaign should plan to build one and maintain it during the 45 to 90 days before election day. For a very low cost, the campaign in support of a district's tax proposal can present a great deal of information. Even if created with limited Web skills, a site can present much more visual information about the benefits of the district's proposal than was ever possible with fliers or mailed media.

The first step in creating a campaign Web site is to pick an appropriate URL (a Uniform Resource Locator). If possible, use the extension .org or .info for your site. Sites that end in .com have become strongly associated with business and commerce. As you evaluate possible URLs, keep in mind that you will invite voters to visit the site in print material, in e-mails, in person, and by phone. Therefore, pick a URL that is easy to remember and *very easy* to spell. Voters will be more likely to remember and spell correctly in their browser www.YesforKids.org than they will www.YesAcalanesYes.org. Although the latter includes the name of the district, not all voters can spell Acalanes easily and quickly. Finally, think about how and where the URL will be disseminated. If the district is going to include it in any of its information materials, do not include the word "yes" in the URL.[1]

What you ultimately place on a campaign Web site is limited only by your imagination, but some basic materials are recommended. Use the home page as a bulletin board that changes regularly to highlight campaign events. It should also have links to pages such as the following:

- A page with the fact sheet that will be printed and distributed as part of the citizens' advocacy campaign. The content of this page will not change once it is posted.
- A more dynamic page where you present the answers to frequently asked questions. Add new questions and answers to this page as the campaign proceeds.
- A page that presents the language voters will actually see on the ballot and that explains what some of the more obscure parts of the text really mean.
- A page where voters can read about and see how their tax dollars will be used, especially if the proposal is for school construction or renovation. This page can include still and video materials depending on the skill of the campaign's Web master.
- A page that provides links to government sites where individuals can register to vote and, if you plan to encourage supporters to vote by mail, a link to a site where they can apply for an absentee ballot.
- A page that makes it easy for voters to see what has been written about the district's proposal, especially if the proposal gets good coverage in the press or is endorsed by the local paper.

- A page that presents all of the endorsements the proposal has received from individuals and groups. This page should also include a way for visitors to endorse the proposal and to volunteer to help in the campaign.

As the Web site is developed, its look and feel should be the same as the designs selected by the campaign for its more traditional voter contact materials. Visitors to the site should easily recognize the site as related to the piece of direct mail they recently received or the door hanger left by a campaign volunteer. Of course, the next challenge the campaign faces is getting that visitor to the Web site.

The first step in this process is to remember to place the site's URL in everything the campaign produces. All of the printed material that is part of a traditional voter contact program needs to promote the site and list the URL. Then begin to plan for the use of many of the other new technology tools available to a school tax campaign to make voters aware of the site and its content.

E-MAIL

E-mail offers the campaign an effective way to inform voters that a Web site exists. As noted in chapter 2, e-mail addresses can be appended to a voter file. These can be used to invite voters to visit the campaign's Web site. Such contact must be targeted in the same way direct mail will be targeted. Depending on how schools and school districts have collected e-mail addresses,[2] it may be possible to e-mail the parent population as soon as the Web site is ready.

If an existing list of parent e-mail addresses is not available, the campaign can begin to collect them by beginning a "viral" e-mail campaign. To execute such a campaign, the core parent volunteers in the campaign should be asked to e-mail a message from the campaign to the parents they know are in their e-mail address books. The content of this e-mail should be developed by the campaign. It should include a link to the page on the Web site where individuals can endorse and leave the campaign an e-mail address. It should also ask the parents who receive the e-mail to forward it to the parents in their address books. Generally, such an e-mail campaign can quickly make contact with a large portion of the parent population and begin to allow the campaign to build its own e-mail list.

Like traditional direct mail, one e-mail is not enough. The campaign should plan a series of e-mails, especially in the 30 to 45 days before election day. Unlike direct mail, these are generally very short and, other than asking voters to go to the Web site and endorse, address a single topic. Some will remind voters of key dates in the election calendar, like the last day a person can register to vote or the last day to apply for an absentee ballot. Others will present one important fact about the proposal and urge the recipient to learn more about that aspect of the proposal by following

GIVE OUR STUDENTS A WORLD-CLASS EDUCATION

Did you know....

Many people in our district believe Zimmerman currently has a dedicated high school?

The upcoming November 6 referendum features a new $51 million dedicated high school for Zimmerman that will include:

- Space to teach 1,000 students;
- Community auditorium;
- Three-station gym;
- Full athletic fields.

The new Zimmerman high school will open with more students than Rogers High School did when it opened in 2000

We need your help to spread the word!

Contact Joe Stangler or Charlie Blesener for ways you can help create Room to Grow, and Space to Learn!

Figure 8.1.   Sample E-mail

a link to a specific point on the campaign Web site. The e-mails developed for the campaign can use simple text, but many campaigns use a service like Constant Contact to send e-mails with the same graphic look and feel as the campaign's Web site and printed materials.

Finally, as e-mails are planned, remember that a campaign can send too many e-mails. When using a service like Constant Contact, monitor the click-through rate for each e-mail sent by the campaign. Checking the click-through rate lets you see how many of the people who received the e-mail opened it and followed one of the links in the e-mail's text. If the click-through rate drops off significantly, the campaign is probably sending too many e-mails.

TEXT MESSAGES

Text messages offer the campaign another way to contact voters—especially young voters. To do so, the campaign will need to build a list of the cell phones of its supporters. This can be done in much the same way the "viral e-mail" campaign started the process of collecting e-mail addresses. Because receiving a text message can cost the recipient something, the campaign should make sure that voters opt into the campaign's message system either through the campaign Web site or by sending a text message to a number supplied by the campaign. By their very nature, these messages are very short. Like e-mails, they can be used to remind voters of key dates in the election calendar (e.g., close of registration). They can and should always invite recipients to visit the campaign's Web site. On election day, they can also be a very effective addition to a campaign's get-out-the-vote effort.[3]

ADWORDS

If the campaign budget can afford it, Google Adwords can also be used to drive visitors to the campaign Web site. Google's Adwords product causes a Google ad to appear when someone searches on a specific word or phrase. If the campaign has established an Adword ad for the phrase "learning levy" that links to the campaign's Web site, that ad will be shown to anyone who searches Google for the same phrase. The ad that appears might say "Support Richfield Schools" or "Support Strong Schools" above a link to the campaign's Web site. The campaign is charged when someone clicks on the ad and is sent to the Web site.

It is best if the link takes individuals to a place on the site not only where they can learn about the district's proposal but also where they are asked to do something. This request can be as simple as giving them an opportunity to ask a question, make a comment, or endorse the proposal.

The key to using Adwords ads is to experiment with variations on the language of the ads associated with each key word. Google provides very good feedback concerning both the number of times the ad is displayed (which tells you if you are using the right key word) and the number of times the ad is clicked on. You can establish an Adwords ad that is visible to the nation, a whole state, or just one city.[4]

VIDEO

If a picture is worth one thousand words, then a moving picture with sound must be worth a million. The evolution of the tools involved in video production—both the handheld video cameras and the software available for editing—means that school tax campaigns can visually present the building or program challenges that caused the district to place a tax proposal on the ballot. The need for additional funds to address renovation and construction proposals can be captured if the camera accompanies a school tour narrated by the principal or superintendent. Overcrowded classrooms and hallways can be captured if the camera follows one or two students as they move from one classroom to another. The need to invest in the talents of this generation of students can be captured by asking 5th- or 6th-grade students to make simple statements about the future: "I will be your doctor" or "I will teach your grandchildren." Once created, a video can be posted to YouTube or a similar site and can be linked to the campaign's Web site. It can also be made into a DVD, copied, and distributed to voters throughout the district.

BLOGS

The term "blog" was derived from the phrase "Web log." Technorati, a group that has been tracking the growth of blogs since 2004, defines a blog as "a Web site, usually maintained by an individual with regular entries of commentary, descriptions of events, or other material such as graphics or video" (http://technorati.com/blogging/state-of-the-blogosphere). Each blog entry is a short statement, and new material needs to be added to the blog on a regular basis. Adding a blog to your campaign will also allow for two-way communication with local voters. Most blogs allow readers to comment and react to the material posted on the blog.

There are two ways to approaching blogging. You can use a blogging service like www.blogger.com or www.blog.com. These sites and others like them are free and make it very easy to set up and maintain a blog. You can also build a blog into your Web site by visiting www.movabletype.com and downloading the software you will need.

Before you post anything to your blog, develop a list of facts about your district's school tax proposal and use this list to develop a blog post calendar. By doing so, you will be ready to regularly post new material to the blog in a logical sequence. Also, decide if you are going to attempt to place limits on who can post material on the blog. A completely open blog will create the greatest amount of work and runs the risk that you will give opponents access to your supporters.

Finally, as you begin to tell voters that the blog exists, you will need to monitor it regularly to make sure that any questions raised on the site are addressed promptly. Remember, everyone on the Internet believes that everything happens instantly.

SOCIAL NETWORKS

Having a presence on MySpace, Facebook, Twitter, or one of the other social networks provides yet another vehicle for communication with voters—especially younger voters. A school district or a campaign establishes a presence, searches for people, and invites them to be "friends," "followers," or "fans." Like the viral e-mail campaign, campaign volunteers should be asked to link the campaign's presence on the social network to their friends. Another very logical use of these networks is to have current high school students work to find recent graduates. As "friends," these recent graduates can be informed of the district's need for funds and urged to cast a vote in support of the district's tax proposal. Like a blog, you can post information as text, a video, or a photograph. As with a blog, you should outline a number of short items you could post and then use that list to create a calendar.

There are differences in how each of these social networks works—and by the time you read this material, they may have changed. As this text is being written, MySpace allows users to modify their presence using HTML code and cascading style sheets (CSS). Until recently, Facebook allowed pictures, video, audio, and text to be posted in an environment that the user cannot modify. Facebook is changing the way in which a school district or campaign could post material to the network. Twitter is even more restrictive, allowing users to post no more than 140 characters at a time. Over time, one can be assured that each of these will continue to change and new social networks will continue to emerge. But as the Iranian election crisis of 2009 made clear, these communications tools have a very important role in modern communications planning.

TELEPHONE CONTACT

Although phone banks have been used for many years to identify support and to remind supporters to vote, there are some new ways to use the phone as part of a school tax campaign. Automated calling—or "robo calls"—can be used to augment live contact with supporters. A recorded message can be delivered to thousands of telephones within a very short timeframe at a very low cost. There are many vendors around the country who can distribute the message for the campaign. The key to making these calls work is to find the appropriate person to deliver the message. For example, a respected community leader or retired principal can increase the attention paid to the message.

Brevity and voice quality are also important. Like e-mail and text messages, these calls can be used to remind supporters of key dates in the election calendar. Whenever a call is made, make sure the message includes a reference to the URL of the campaign's Web site. One caveat: in some states, robo calls are illegal. Also, federal statutes require that these calls identify who has initiated the call and offer a way to contact that organization. Many states also have laws that impose additional restrictions or prohibit these calls completely. Be sure to check the laws in your state before planning to add this voter contact tool to your campaign.

TELEPHONE TOWN HALL MEETING

The telephone can be used to hold a "virtual" town hall meeting. This type of call functions like a talk radio program that is conducted via a community-wide conference call. An invitation to participate is recorded and a target audience is selected from the voters with available phone numbers. Using the same technology as the robo call, the invitation is delivered to the target audience very rapidly. As residents answer the phone, they hear a version of the invitation that invites them to stay on the line as the call is transferred into the virtual town hall meeting if they want to participate. If the invitation is delivered to an answering machine, the message can contain instructions about how one can join the call by dialing a toll-free number.

In the virtual town hall meeting, a moderator and two or three hosts are available to discuss the district's tax proposal and to answer questions from participants. For a school tax proposal, the hosts will often be some combination of the superintendent, a board member, a principal, or a parent leader. To prepare for this type of meeting, a minute-by-minute timeline should be developed, outlining what the moderator and hosts will talk about while waiting for one of the participants to ask a question. Participants press one of the keys on their phone to indicate they have a question and are then sent to a call screener. The screener places the caller in line for the moderator to introduce to the meeting and provides the moderator with a short description of the participant's question. This process allows one of the hosts to prepare to answer the question.

As with robo calls, there are many vendors around the country capable of providing this service. Once the meeting is over, most provide a complete audio recording of the meeting. To allow others to benefit from the questions asked and answers provided during the meeting, audio excerpts can—and should—be posted on the campaign's Web site.

Using this technology to reach out to the community and discuss a proposal is much more efficient than the process of holding public meetings at school sites and will most likely engage more people than the traditional town hall forum. A district might hold a virtual town hall meeting with the parent population as the proposal is being shaped and considered by the administration and the school board. A campaign might hold this type of meeting after its voter contact campaign has started in order to answer questions about the district's proposal.

WHICH TOOLS ARE RIGHT FOR YOUR CAMPAIGN?

Just because all of the new technologies presented here exist and have been used in campaigns does not mean your campaign needs to harness them all to be successful. Using any of these tools will require volunteer time, some demand unique volunteer skills and experience, and for others cost may be prohibitive. Plan to add these tools to your campaign after determining that you can very effectively use them as part of your voter contact effort. A good campaign executes the limited number of steps included in its campaign plan completely and effectively. A poorly managed campaign tries to do everything and, usually, fails to fully and effectively complete any part of the campaign.

NOTES

1. Including a reference to a campaign Web site in district material is something that should be reviewed by the district's lawyers.

2. Accessing and using parent e-mail addresses is another thing that should be reviewed by the district's lawyers.

3. Adding text messages can be done by using vendors that have added SMS text messaging to the voter contact services they offer. One such vendor can be found at www.mcsphones.com.

4. The campaign can control the cost of launching an Adwords campaign. There is no cost involved in setting it up, and when one is created, the campaign defines how much it wants to pay Google when someone clicks on an ad. Typical costs range from 25¢ to 50¢ per click-through. In addition, an Adwords campaign can specify a maximum the campaign wants to spend per month.

9

Planning

If you skipped to this chapter to review our suggested campaign plan, turn back to the beginning of the book and start reading. Every part of this book is designed to help you plan and execute a successful campaign in your school district. It does not, however, contain a copy of "The Doctors' Patented Winning Campaign Plan." The reason is simple: no single plan can meet the needs of *every* school district and *every* election environment. But there is a process that will allow you to create a winning plan for your district.

The process of writing a complete campaign plan will be one of the most overwhelming tasks a school leader will ever undertake. Even when a district brings in professional consulting for guidance through the process of planning and executing a school tax campaign, the process is one that demands all of the time, energy, and talent school leaders have to offer. Preparing for, planning, and executing a campaign must, if done properly, distract the superintendent, the school board, key staff, and parents from the tasks they perform during a normal school year.

The process of successfully planning and executing a campaign actually has a great deal in common with the tasks surrounding the preparation of Thanksgiving dinner. If you routinely plan and cook Thanksgiving dinner so that everything arrives on the table hot, handsomely presented, and cooked to perfection while the guests take their seats just as the last of the serving dishes are placed on the table, you have an understanding of the skills it takes to plan and execute a school tax campaign. And, just as you spent time learning the techniques of preparing this annual family feast from parents and relatives, you need to take time now to learn an approach to campaign planning that will give you the necessary tools to create a winning campaign plan.

BASIC RULES

Before beginning a discussion of our approach to planning, let us look at some of the basic rules that apply to all school tax campaigns. These rules will apply throughout the planning process. Although following all of them will not guarantee you a victory, ignoring them will ensure a loss.

- *Start planning early*. If you are reading this book in January and know your district will place a proposal on the November ballot, do not put the book down and figure you will start applying what you have learned closer to election day. Given all that must be done to fully prepare a school district for a school tax campaign, January is awfully close—maybe too close—to November. In most cases, give yourself at least 12 months. And remember that vacation schedules make the summer a very difficult time to get anything done. Never assume you will get half of what you planned to do on the campaign done between June and September.
- *Make sure the campaign plan coordinates the activities of the school district and the citizens' campaign*. The laws of each state place various restrictions on district activities. But throughout the planning process, you are creating a unified campaign in which the district and citizens will have clearly defined, coordinated roles.
- *Review all district policies that may impact the ability of your campaign to develop*. These may include data privacy policies or the manner in which parent e-mail addresses are collected.
- *Find and use outside talent where it will expand the expertise found in your district office and school buildings*. A school tax election will require the school district to use skills and talents that are not a part of its regular operations. While no district's budget is unlimited, long experience has taught us that a school tax election is not the time or place to be penny wise and pound foolish. A wise district starts early in assembling the team that will help it plan and execute a victory at the ballot box.

Building Your Team

- *Make sure you have the legal and financial help you need.* Even though the district has lawyers and financial planners who help with day-to-day operations, the district will need to consult lawyers and financial advisors who specialize in school tax proposals. Lawyers who specialize in school tax proposals will provide you with the legal deadlines with which you must comply and an outline of the legal documents that must be prepared before you can go onto the ballot. Financial advisors can provide you with accurate estimates of how much the proposal will cost the average voter in the district.

- *Consult with outside architects and engineers.* In many districts, the facilities department is quite capable of describing and documenting the challenges facing the districts classrooms and buildings. It is important to have this work checked and rechecked, however, by outside architects and engineers familiar with the questions voters will ask the district once a proposal is placed on the ballot.

- *Realize curriculum review is an ongoing process.* Preparation for a campaign may require the district to bring in outside facilitators to expand the normal review process to include an attempt to quantify and make specific the district's vision of the classroom education it wants to provide in the future.

- *Hire communications and community research specialists.* Although the district may have excellent communications and assessment departments, there are communications and community research specialists who work almost exclusively with school tax proposals. Do not hesitate to learn from them how survey research and communications planning differ when the goal is a "yes" vote on a local proposal.

- *Seek out campaign consultants who can assist in the process of turning your desire to address a financial challenge or improve your schools into a concrete plan for winning on election day.* Such a consultant should never replace the army of school people you will need to win, but his or her understanding of how to structure a campaign can save you the time you might otherwise spend "reinventing the wheel."

- *If a campaign plan is not written down, it does not exist.*

Now let's look at several frameworks for examining your district's situation and creating a campaign plan that will meet your specific needs. If your district has never been on the ballot, this process will help you think through all of the steps involved in creating an effective, winning plan for your first campaign. If you have campaigned before and lost, it should help you look at your district, its needs, and your community in a different way. In *Reframing Organizations*, Bolman and Deal (1991) introduce four "lenses" or "frames" for organizational analysis:

- Structural.
- Human resource.
- Political.
- Symbolic.

Viewing your situation through these lenses and approaching the next election with this framework in mind can help you engage in the process of winning with an integrated, comprehensive plan.

THE STRUCTURAL FRAME

The structural frame relates to coordinating, organizing, controlling, planning, goal setting, and clarifying expectations. From this, strategies develop. If this is your district's first referendum effort, use all of the data available in an annotated voter file and in demographic district maps to understand *who* the voters in your district are. There will be key questions to answer. Are district parents registered to vote? If they are registered, do they participate or does it take a presidential election to get most of them to the polls? Does the ethnic background of your student and parent population match that of the population of registered voters? Very often, district leadership is surprised to find that although more than half of their students are from minority populations, minorities still make up a small percentage of the voting population in the district. If your district has been on the ballot sometime during the last few years, expand your knowledge of the voters in the district by completing a post-election analysis. Learn everything possible about your district through the statistics that define it and its voting population.

Expand what you have learned by using survey research where appropriate to explore the degree to which the community around you understands the challenges facing the district and shares your goals for the future. These research tools will allow you to develop a clear understanding of the community's core values. You can then work to present the community with a school tax proposal that is well aligned with their expectations.

Fully evaluate all district communications by asking someone from outside the district to review the materials you have been producing. Work with your state's public relations association or a private consultant to understand which parts of your current communications program are working and, most important, which are not. During this process, it is very important to find those places in your communications where you are using educational jargon. Though such language is extremely useful as you communicate with colleagues and peers, it may not communicate your challenges, goals, and solutions effectively to the broader community. One district, for example, delivered a very high-quality, child-centered education, but a review of their communications found that the materials never used the words *child* or *children*. By making a conscious effort to use those words thereafter, they made their communication much more effective.

As you learn more about your district, use this material to write a detailed and comprehensive plan. Capture details about the challenges you face. If you cannot quantify the ways in which additional tax funds will be spent, add to your timeline the steps needed to complete a facilities audit or curriculum review. After an evaluation of district communications, outline the steps that will be required to improve the program's effectiveness. Following the creation of an annotated voter file and, possibly, post-election analysis, determine whether parents within the district are registered and whether they vote. If they are not voters, make sure the plan includes ways to increase parental registration and participation. If there are areas of the district that may oppose—or always have opposed—school taxes, make sure the plan captures your best thoughts and ideas about how you will overcome these potential "no" votes. When the plan is finished, move on to recruit capable people to execute it.

THE HUMAN RESOURCE FRAME

The human resource frame relates to involving people through an understanding of each individual's feelings, needs, preferences, abilities, and desire for participation. Begin with an honest evaluation of the leadership being provided by the school board, superintendent, administrators, teachers, staff, and parent volunteers. Evaluate that leadership as it applies to the events of the current school year and then look into the district's past. Base the evaluation of the leadership available in the district on qualitative and quantitative data. A realistic assessment of the leadership resources available in your district will have a direct impact on the success of the campaign and the district's ability to meet the need of students through the ballot proposal.

Just as there are professionals who can help you review district communications, there are professionals who specialize in helping school districts plan and execute school tax campaigns. Do not hesitate to bring these consultants into the district to assist in the evaluation of your leadership resources. Because they have gone through the process of planning and executing school tax campaigns more times than any superintendent ever could, they can offer valuable insight into the human resources available in your district. They also can provide invaluable support as you work to motivate your election team and win your campaign.

As you work to identify and solicit leadership for your campaign, use the *ideal task performer* philosophy. No matter what job there is to be done, there is an ideal task performer to do it. Think for a moment about two jobs that almost every campaign has: someone who coordinates the activities of the campaign volunteers and someone who actively recruits those volunteers. If two people have expressed an interest in these jobs, the campaign will most likely be best served if the detail-oriented introvert takes on the role of coordinator while the extroverted chair of the PTA takes on the job of recruiting people to work in the campaign. The more critical the task, the more important it is to find ideal task performers.

Pay special attention to the verbs that were just used. Leadership will be *identified*, *solicited*, and *recruited*. This process involves work and time, all of which must be accounted for in your campaign plan. Many campaigns end the night the superintendent or school board president calls a meeting in the gym to ask if anyone would like to chair the district's upcoming school tax campaign. The approach we are recommending strongly suggests that developing a leadership team is both strategic and "hands on" and discards the notion that the superintendent would call a meeting in the school cafeteria to find volunteers to chair the campaign. Identifying, soliciting, and recruiting the leadership needed for a campaign is a process. Provide time for it in your campaign plan and define the specific steps you will need to take to complete it. And remember that all leaders—whether staff, parent volunteers, or community members—must also be chosen with a keen sense of how they will be perceived by the public.

In addition to leaders, every campaign needs volunteers. The best campaigns apply Tom Sawyer's philosophy and involve a lot of people. If five volunteers might complete the job of canvassing a neighborhood near the district office, recruit 10. For every job where it makes sense, involve as many people as possible. Their involvement will make light work of many of the campaign's most difficult or mundane tasks. In addition, the more that teachers, staff, and parents invest in the campaign—both through the hours they volunteer and the dollars they donate—the more likely they are to remember to end the campaign by casting a ballot. As you develop a campaign plan, quantify your need for volunteer hours and list the ways in which volunteers will be recruited.

Difficult and Mundane?

Not all tasks that must be completed to win a campaign are exciting. A sign used to hang in the Government Relations office of one of the nation's largest teacher organizations. It read: "Campaigns take the brightest, most energetic people in your organization and ask them to complete the most boring, mundane tasks they can imagine."

THE POLITICAL FRAME

The political frame focuses on the conflict, negotiations, influence, and interplay among different constituencies, interest groups, and organizations. This frame will include how you approach the leaders of the political parties in your community and how you plan to make contact with those groups of voters that your post-election analysis, demographic mapping, and community survey tell you are most likely to resist your effort to raise taxes. Begin with the positive by identifying community VIPs and soliciting their opinions and support. Seek out "blockbuster" endorsements, especially from individuals who "everyone" might assume will oppose your school tax proposal. If you have been on the ballot and lost, this will include looking for converts who will change from a public "no" to a public "yes."

Often as a school leader, you are not in a position to directly influence the members of the community most likely to oppose you. But that does not mean you cannot reach out and ask for the help of supporters who can influence those groups or individuals. For example, a district that lost two school tax elections knew that its proposal failed due to an antitax vote in the community. No argument the school community made concerning the need for classroom programs and well-maintained buildings influenced the leaders of these antitax voters. Before its next election, the district solicited and received the support of members of the business community. With their help, they built a strong case for the school tax around the idea that local property values were being threatened by a weakened school district. This argument, presented with the help of the local business community, was able to influence some of the antitax voters, thus reducing the number of "no" votes cast to the point that the district passed its proposal.

A second example involved some background research. A school district lost a major school tax election because of the outspoken opposition of the local taxpayers association. After the loss, district leadership brought in the help it needed to assess the funding sources that were supporting the taxpayers' groups. Once identified, the district was able to talk with supporters who worked for many of the companies that were supplying the taxpayers with campaign funds. Those employees were able to slow down and in some cases stop the flow of funding to the taxpayers after they talked to their bosses and coworkers about what the loss meant to classroom programs throughout the district. As you develop a campaign plan, think about ways that you can convert or isolate potential opponents. Quantify the steps involved and provide ample time in your campaign calendar.

The political framework also demands that you be very clear about how a loss impacts the community and its children. All school tax campaigns live with some built-in limitations. You cannot build your campaign on the threat that a loss will mean that you will shut down the entire 3rd grade. School leaders, principals, and teachers will do everything in their power to keep schools and classrooms open regardless of how much funding the legislature or the community takes away. But as it approaches a campaign, district leadership must be willing to state very clearly the consequences of winning or losing on election day. Thinking through those consequences and writing them down are essential to planning. You must identify what is at risk and you must be willing to tell people that their vote will make a difference. You cannot exaggerate because school will be open on the day after the election and the community will see what happens. People will not vote "yes," however, if doing so *might* or *could* or *probably* or *maybe* will cause something to happen. Be clear and firm.

Explore opportunities to use cognitive dissonance and remove anger in the community. Cognitive dissonance reflects an internal struggle within the voter between a historical tendency to vote "no" and an emerging attitude of support. The dictionary definition of dissonance is "discord." In music, dissonance is a combination of tones that are not harmonious and suggest an unrelieved tension. Cognitive dissonance is a thought process that attempts to reconcile an internal conflict or paradox in one's mind. In finance elections, cognitive dissonance is created when conflict and uncertainty exist within individuals or groups that might typically be expected to oppose the election. For example, retired voters living on fixed incomes will be conservative and overrepresented among "no" voters. Inviting senior citizens to volunteer and participate in the schools will not only create a bridge to seniors but will create cognitive dissonance.

Likewise, asking retirees who are supportive of the district's proposal to present it to other groups of older voters will have a much more meaningful impact than a presentation by campaign chairs 20 or 30 years younger than anyone in the audience. Finally, asking the assistance of service groups such as the American Legion to help with Flag Day observances not only connects them to children but also creates questions about the consequences of voting against educational funding. Cognitive dissonance may not change a "no" vote to a "yes" vote, but it will give reason to question the opposition and de-energize detractors, who, rather than voting "no," may choose not to vote at all.

THE SYMBOLIC FRAME

The symbolic lens provides a view of the "meaning" of the campaign and presents standards for the participants to rally around. The symbolic presentation of the core issues in the campaign is important whether you plan to try to "fly below the radar" or to take your campaign down the middle of Main Street with drums beating and flags flying. How you translate the need for your school tax proposal into a statement that conveys both meaning and emotion is extremely important.

Since the only thing that will win a "yes" vote from the average voter is information about the need for the school tax proposal, all campaigns produce large quantities of written material. A two-page fact sheet may accompany a short letter outlining the need for the school tax proposal. Voters still needing more information will be offered a page of frequently asked questions or invited to visit the campaign's Web site on which every possible piece of persuasive information has been accumulated. But as these materials are created, they must convey more than the words they contain. At every opportunity, the words must be delivered in a package that will visually rally the reader to the district's cause. The choice of colors and photographs as well as the careful, artistic manner in which materials are laid out and typeset and even the paper selected for printing can help to emphasize the need for the school tax proposal.

One district developed a very detailed, written fact sheet that it planned to distribute to all voters in the community. Using an annotated voter file, it was able to divide the voter file into three parts: parents, voters who were 65 or older, and nonparent voters younger than 65. Using exactly the same text, it created three versions of the fact sheet—each designed for use with a specific audience. The version sent to parents used photographs of parents interacting with classroom teachers and young children to emphasize the content of the piece. The fact sheet sent to older voters used pictures of grandparents volunteering in the classroom and reading to young children. For the younger nonparent audience, a photograph depicted a young couple interacting with their neighbors and their neighbors' children. In the background, a strategically placed For Sale sign adorned a lawn across the street. The visual materials added to each version of the fact sheet helped reinforce its message with its specific audience. Therefore, campaign planning will require that you not only outline the prose you need to write to present the school tax proposal to the community—it will require you to think of the ways in which that prose will be presented.

You will also need to think through the "theater" associated with media contact during your campaign. A dry presentation of enrollment statistics and projections may convince the press your schools are overcrowded, but creatively placing a news reporter in an overcrowded portable classroom for a day may help to emphasize the point. However, photo opportunities should never be staged. If you pack 53 students into one classroom only for the hour the reporter could visit, someone will inevitably find out. Nevertheless, when you provide information to the media, remember to do so with a symbolic framework that emphasizes the "rightness" of your campaign.

Two examples will help illustrate. After a very painful series of public meetings to cut the budget, one district was finally ready for the school board meeting during which a multimillion-dollar budget cut would be approved. Because the earlier meetings were exhausting and the subject was painful, no one from the district or board thought to ask any parents or teachers to attend the meeting. When the final vote came, the only person to speak was a retiree who thought more cuts ought to be made in the administration. As a result, instead of covering the cuts themselves, the media focused on the fact that more might have been done. This district forgot to surround its very difficult vote with an appropriate touch of theater. The delivery of the district's message would have improved if even a handful of parents spoke to the fact that these difficult cuts were going to have a serious impact on the students, district, and community.

The second example concerns the selection of appropriate theater. A district that needed to build more classrooms staged a press conference at the school they thought best for an outdoor news event. It had a large bus turnaround, an ample front lawn, good short-term parking on the streets in front of the school for the media, and a good view of the growing number of portable classrooms being packed onto the school's athletic fields. Unfortunately, it was also a middle school. As the campaign chairs diligently presented the reasons a school bond was needed, the media became more fascinated with the antics of the middle school students assembled behind the speakers. Good actors know they never want to be upstaged by a baby, a dog, or a group of middle school students.

The process of evaluating the symbolic presentation of the campaign becomes increasingly important *if* a school tax campaign chooses to become more visible. If a campaign is to become more visible, the campaign's symbols must compellingly and clearly build support for the proposal. Before continuing, however, we must digress. The word *if* was carefully chosen here. Buttons, signs, and banners all have a place in school tax campaigns. Each should be evaluated as part of the symbolic presentation of the campaign to the community. Often circumstances will dictate a campaign abandon any hope of "flying beneath the radar" and incorporate these more visible campaign tools. Two rules, however, should govern the use of such materials:

- *Can the campaign afford them?* If the campaign decides to use its available communications funds to buy buttons instead of printing its fact sheet, the campaign is headed in the wrong direction. People must have information; therefore, unless you have very large buttons available, campaign dollars must be used for fact sheets long before they are used for buttons.
- *Will they provide the school tax campaign with a distinct advantage over those inclined to vote "no" or are you doing this because "every campaign" does?* If a district knows that it will be faced with a very visible opposition campaign, then going public in a big way has some distinct advantages. A massive display of buttons and signs can give the undecided a reason to vote "yes" and, if you are lucky, "no" voters a reason to switch as they see the breadth of support for the schools and community. If, however, there will be no visible opposition, a massive display of signs and banners may only serve to remind the "no" voters to cast their ballots on election day. Every action the campaign takes needs to be evaluated to ensure it is clearly an action advantageous to the process of winning "yes" votes.

These four frameworks provide you with a way to begin to evaluate and quantify the specific challenges, resources, and strengths your district brings to a campaign. Writing the plan (remember, *writing* is the key word here) will demand that all of your thoughts and ideas be captured, evaluated, and defined in terms of volunteers needed, steps to completion, time required for each task, and impact of every activity under consideration. Campaigns should not attempt to complete every task they have ever seen used in other campaigns. Rather, you need to identify those that will work in your district on the ballot you have selected for your school tax proposal. The end results will be detailed timelines and task descriptions that will take your district through months of preparation and approximately 10 weeks of active, public campaigning on your way to a win on election day.

10

Leadership and Organization

Successful finance elections require strong leadership and effective organization. Using a military analogy, winning campaigns require a great battle plan; a professional, experienced general; precise execution by subordinates in the field; and strong logistical support. As generals morph to superintendents, however, the research is mixed in terms of how to best lead and organize a successful school finance campaign. Three constants apply to all school districts:

- The campaign must have strong leadership.
- The campaign must be well organized.
- The campaign must identify and recruit the ideal task performers for each and every leadership function.

Within this context there are important roles for the superintendent, school board, staff, parent leaders, and volunteers that play out similarly in most school communities.

ROLE OF THE SCHOOL BOARD

The school board's crucial role is one of the most often-tested variables in scholarly research and the most consistent in how it correlates with successful elections. Simply put, achieving and maintaining a unanimous, supportive, and engaged school board may be the campaign's most important asset. More than one researcher has warned against moving forward on a school finance election until this is achieved. The margins between winning and losing are just too slim to give wary taxpayers an excuse to vote "no" as a result of a split, schizophrenic, or vacillating school board that is unable to get its act together.

Although campaign laws vary as to the extent to which school board members may participate as advocates during a school finance election, it is generally a misconception that board members cannot or should not be supportive and engaged. In most states, individual board members—operating independently from their official duties—are free to volunteer their time and support to a campaign. The community's culture, survey results, and perception of school board members—individually and collectively—will dictate the optimal visibility of their roles. In conceptualizing the role of the school board, campaign planners should focus on the following key functions before and during the campaign:

- Maintaining a focus on student needs.
- Polling community opinions before final ballot decisions.
- Providing a unanimous resolution to conduct the election.
- Aligning the final proposal with the community's values and its appetite for spending.
- Involving citizens in the campaign.
- Providing support to the administration and volunteer committee.

ROLE OF THE SUPERINTENDENT

The superintendent's vital role is to either provide the needed leadership, planning, and expertise *or* ensure that someone else does it effectively. As noted previously, university libraries are replete with research focused on the variables affecting the outcomes of school finance elections. Additionally, empirical data—capturing the latest strategies and techniques used by successful school districts—should be collected and analyzed. Similar to the role of any successful CEO, the superintendent must provide the leadership, direction, and strategic planning necessary to achieve the organization's priorities—in this case a successful bond or operating election.

Equally important, once the course is set, someone must ensure the plan is executed at the highest level. Who provides this critical leadership—whether it's the superintendent or a designee—will vary depending on many factors, including the size of the district and the viability of the current superintendent. Key functions performed by the superintendent before and during the campaign include:

- Planning strategically and meticulously based on research and best practice.
- Working closely with the advocacy campaign to execute, monitor, and coordinate efforts.
- Knowing when to use experts to supplement local resources.
- Obtaining support and participation from staff in cooperation with the campaign committee.
- Providing information, support, and resources to the campaign committee within the parameters of state law.

ROLE OF FACULTY AND STAFF

Another mistake is to conclude that faculty and staff members cannot or should not be involved in advocacy roles in support of a school finance campaign. While school leaders certainly need to address this issue within the context of their state's election laws, faculty and staff generally are free to express and exercise their political rights. In fact, in most communities, visible and strong support from teachers, secretaries, custodians, and bus drivers will be an asset to the campaign. Conversely, the damage can be significant when large numbers of employees criticize the ballot proposal, how the school district has used money in the past, or the performance of the school board, superintendent, or staff. Equally troubling to the campaign are staff members who are unable to answer even basic questions posed by friends or neighbors. Although these problems are not fully under the school district's or campaign's control, they can be minimized by focusing on the needs of employees and investing in them in terms of providing information and responding to questions and concerns.

In the final analysis, those individuals ultimately responsible for campaign strategy and planning need to determine the optimal involvement of faculty and staff based on the culture within the community and how individuals and groups are generally perceived. Key functions of faculty and staff before and during a school finance campaign include:

- Solidifying and strengthening relationships with primary constituency (i.e., parents).
- Identifying ways to reach out and enhance secondary constituencies within the community.
- Demonstrating good stewardship of what has already been provided.
- Asking questions and staying informed.
- Supporting and participating in the campaign.

ROLE OF CITIZENS' CAMPAIGN COMMITTEE

Unlike the school board, which has a responsibility to inform all constituents of the district's proposal, citizens involved in the campaign are driven by an advocacy mission focused on persuading as many residents as possible to cast "yes" votes on election day. The role of the campaign committee is fundamentally political in nature and, like any political campaign, should focus on making its case, identifying support, and motivating the right voters to get to the polls. Therefore, all registered voters should not be treated the same in terms of communications and get-out-the-vote strategies.

One of the biggest challenges—and often the Achilles' heel of unsuccessful campaigns—is a lack of consistency in message and poor coordination between the school district and campaign committee. For example, if the district can legally mail information to the community, launching door-to-door or phone canvassing before the school district mails residents information does not build goodwill or better friendships within the school community. (*Note*: The laws of each state differ concerning the degree to which school districts can distribute information once a proposal is placed on the ballot. As part of the planning process, make sure you understand all of the laws that might restrict district activity.)

Problems can be minimized or avoided by developing an integrated election plan that incorporates both school district and campaign tasks and timelines in one master-planning document. They can also be addressed by including the superintendent and school board chairperson on the campaign committee as ex-officio participants. The remainder of the school board can serve in similar roles on the campaign's working committees. The citizens' campaign committee's key responsibilities include:

- Identifying an overall theme as well as core and subordinate messages.
- Gaining influential support.
- Strategically canvassing the community to identify probable "yes" voters.
- Recruiting volunteers for leadership roles.
- Implementing a campaign plan as directed by leadership.
- Coordinating campaign activities with school district initiatives.

School boards, superintendents, staff, and leaders of the citizens' campaign committee almost always perform key roles in campaign planning and execution. This plays out very differently in various school communities, however, and must be evaluated based on local norms, the community's history and culture, and how well these players are perceived within the community. As this relates to the school districts in particular, one way to achieve the best alignment between individuals and groups is to test community perceptions in a pre-election survey before finalizing roles and responsibilities. Consider the example in table 10.1 of data that could be collected within the context of a broader community survey in preparation for a school finance election.

In the District 1 example, the superintendent's performance was rated positively (i.e., excellent or good) by five respondents for every one who rated it as fair or poor. Likewise, the superintendent had high trust levels in District 1. In District 2, however, less than half of the respondents thought the superintendent was doing a good job, with similarly poor marks on trust. In communities like District 1 in the example, the superintendent can and should be the campaign's standard-bearer. In districts like District 2, however, the superintendent would probably best serve the campaign in the background and let other leaders be in the spotlight.

Carefully planned questions within the context of a broader community survey provide the campaign with a significant resource from which to

Table 10.1. Community Perceptions of a School District

How would you rate the overall performance of the following individuals and groups within your local school district?

Key Players	District 1	District 2
Superintendent	5/1	3/4
School Board	5/1	1/1
Principals	3/1	3/2
Teachers	6/1	3/1

To what extent do you trust the credibility and information from the following individuals or groups?

Key Players	District 1	District 2
Superintendent	5/1	2/3
School Board	6/1	1/1
Principals	3/1	4/3
Teachers	8/1	2/1

Note: The numerical ratings represent positive to negative ratios.

link key tasks with ideal task performers. Collecting this kind of information before the election also creates a potential opportunity for the school board and superintendent to proactively work on those issues negatively affecting the public's perception.

IDEAL TASK PERFORMERS

Once the school district and campaign have coordinated election plans, are clear on roles and responsibilities, and understand the appropriate roles of key players, it is time to translate the requirements of the plan into an organizational framework and begin the process of recruiting individuals to fill crucial leadership roles. Chapter 11 presents a prototype for an organizational structure, including a description of working committees and critical responsibilities. It is important to note that there is no right way to organize, and no particular structure will guarantee success. What is fundamentally important to any organizational paradigm, however, is the notion of an *ideal task performer* when it comes to filling leadership roles on the citizens' committee. For many campaigns, failing to do this is not only a missed opportunity but also a fatal mistake.

Efforts to match the right people to the right job run the gambit from laissez faire to surgically precise. At the laissez-faire end of the continuum, imagine a group of community members piling into the high school auditorium for the first planning meeting. As people find their chairs, someone stands, clears her throat, and says, "Who wants to be in charge of finances?" At the surgically precise end of the continuum, a small group of key leaders completes a task analysis of each leadership role and strategically assesses the essential requirements and skills of each leadership position. This approach is reinforced by a core value that the campaign's mission is far too important to settle for anyone but the best.

What is the profile of an ideal task performer? Seeking the following characteristics will aid in focusing your recruitment efforts:

- High level of credibility and respect.
- Well known with a following or network.
- Expertise and experience matched to the leadership role or task.
- Interest in the task at hand.
- Activist and doer.
- Problem solver.

Once your optimal "dream team" is identified on paper, you need to be equally strategic in how to get your prime recruit to "sign on the dotted line." One of the most effective techniques—adapted from social psychology—is to use triangulation (i.e., two individuals approaching a third person). One point of the triangle is a campaign volunteer who has already said "yes" to the committee's call to leadership. The second point of the triangle is the one person your prime recruit simply could not say "no" to when asked to serve. The third point of the triangle is the ideal task performer who is being recruited for a specific function on the committee. This commonsense approach is consistent with our life experiences; it does make a difference who asks us for something and it is more difficult to say "no" to two people rather than one.

Bottom line? You are going for the "Wow!" factor when the community discovers who is actively working on the citizens' campaign committee. Once the leadership team is identified and trained, it is time to execute a winning campaign.

11

Executing the Campaign

In chapter 10, we spotlighted key roles of the school board, superintendent, faculty, and staff, in addition to those of the citizens' campaign committee. Preparing for effective leadership and organization requires a clear understanding of roles, meticulous planning, and the ability to identify and successfully recruit ideal task performers for the campaign. The first element in executing the campaign—the focus of this chapter—is deploying the leaders you have recruited for each and every leadership position within the campaign structure. It should be noted that there is no "right way" to design your campaign structure. The number of committees, committee functions, and how they all tie together in the execution phase will vary based on what has worked in the past. Although your campaign structure will probably be different from what is presented in this chapter, one set of common elements should be a part of *every* campaign.

The campaign structure proposed in this chapter begins with a *steering committee* made up of three community leaders (tri-chairs), the superintendent, and the school board chairperson (see figure 11.1). Although the superintendent and board chairperson play pivotal roles on the steering committee, it is best to keep a strong community face on the campaign by having staff support but not serve in one of the tri-chair positions. The steering committee's primary responsibility is to oversee execution of the campaign plan and six functional committees. Command control in this model is vested in the steering committee as it oversees the campaign activities of the six working committees. The steering committee also must

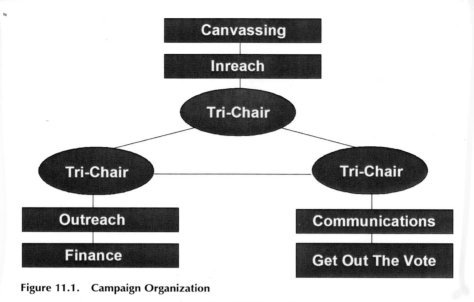

Figure 11.1.   Campaign Organization

ensure that the school district's informational strategies are in sync with the citizens' committee's advocacy efforts.

Although our model depicts tri-chairs, the number of overall campaign leaders should vary depending on the school district's size and demography. For example, a school community with three precincts or wards might best be served with tri-chairs while a district encompassing four independent cities might decide to go with quad-chairs. In a school district in which the district boundaries are coterminous with those of one city, the campaign might deploy anywhere from three to six overall leaders depending on what groups within the community need representation (e.g., parents, senior citizens, business leaders, or civic groups).

In addition to the steering committee members, six committees round out the core campaign and execute the following functions:

- Communication.
- Outreach.
- Inreach.
- Canvassing.
- Finance.
- Get-out-the-vote efforts.

For each of the six committees, we recommend identifying co-chairs—again, parent and community leaders rather than staff—to divide the responsibility and workload (thus making it easier to recruit volunteers to leadership positions) and to broaden the number of individuals involved in the campaign. In addition to the steering committee and co-chairs of the six committees, we recommend including a teacher leader and principal. Depending on how many community leaders are selected for the steering committee, most campaigns using this model end up with a steering committee of five to eight individuals and a total of 18 to 20 members on the broader campaign committee.

Our proposed campaign organization structure also lends itself to effectively involving school board members in the campaign. School board members are often unsure how to best engage and be supportive without overstepping their appropriate role or losing the community "face" of the citizens' campaign. One way to achieve both goals is to ask each of your school board members to serve on one of the six working committees in an ex-officio capacity.[1] By doing so, school board members can show interest and provide support while functioning as information conduits between the campaign and the full school board. Additionally, we recommend district staff be assigned to serve as contacts for each of the six committees to the extent that committee co-chairs have questions or need information.

The remainder of this chapter highlights the key responsibilities and tasks of the steering committee and six working committees.

STEERING COMMITTEE

As stated previously, the campaign's steering committee represents command control. This leadership role begins broadly at a strategic level as the superintendent works closely with citizen leaders to present and discuss election research, survey results, community norms and history, and unique circumstances supporting the strategic plan for the school tax election. The steering committee also plays a pivotal role in luring ideal task performers to leadership positions on the six working committees. Once the campaign leadership roles are fully staffed, the tri-chairs work closely with the superintendent to ensure that vital campaign activities are done well, on time, and in coordination with the school district's information campaign.

Key Steering Committee Responsibilities

The steering committee (i.e., tri-chairs, superintendent, and school board chairperson) functions as central command for executing the campaign. The key responsibilities of the steering committee are:

- Gaining influential support.
- Identifying a target number of identified "yes" voters and concentric voter targets.
- Identifying an overall campaign theme, subordinate themes, and target audiences.
- Determining a budget to support campaign plan.
- Recruiting volunteers for campaign leadership positions.
- Implementing a campaign plan and overseeing activities of volunteers and six working committees.
- Coordinating campaign activities with school district initiatives.

A common problem for both the steering committee and school district is to manage expectations of the school board, internal staff, and volunteers in the face of the campaign's continually changing landscape. Suppose, for example, the school district's ballot proposal seeks to build a new middle school, but with five weeks left until election day, there is a letter to the editor in the local newspaper suggesting the district build a new high school instead. Later that week, similar comments are aired at a public meeting. What to do?

The answer, of course, is the one thing no superintendent or campaign leader wants to hear—it depends! What we *can* provide in the way of guidance, however, is a set of questions and a general recommendation. When faced with this unwanted distraction, the steering committee should ask the following:

- How long is it until election day? Assuming the high school issue is a ripple and not a tidal wave, the closer it is to election day, the easier it is to ignore the issue.

- What kind of margins was the district working with at the start of the campaign based on the survey results (i.e., initial support versus opposition)?
- How credible are the individuals raising the issue?
- How rational or compelling is the argument for a high school rather than a middle school?
- What did the survey say about how most voters get their information about the school district (i.e., how widely read is the newspaper in which the letter to the editor appeared)?
- How has the canvassing been going in terms of identifying support? Is this issue coming up during door-to-door or phone canvassing?

The answers to these questions will help the steering committee and district understand what, if anything, needs to be done to counter what could be a troublesome turn of events. If the steering committee concludes a response is necessary, the ideal task performer strategy should be used to identify *who* should respond. This is also the time to dust off the 80/20 block-and-parry strategy. In other words, when your rebuttal hits the street, it should respond only briefly to the high school argument, saving the heavy ammunition to emphasize and repeat the campaign's core messages for a new middle school delivered in clear, concise, and compelling language.

As for a general recommendation, our experience suggests that if a steering committee looks back after the fact and concludes the high school issue was mishandled, it is more likely the campaign overreacted and lost focus as opposed to not doing enough. It is human nature to be concerned about and feel a need to react to criticism and arguments not supporting the ballot question. It is vitally important, however, to resist being pulled unnecessarily off course and distracted from the mission. Although it is certainly prudent to respond aggressively in some situations, the campaign usually will be better served by sticking to the message and redoubling efforts to communicate core and subordinate messages to the right voters. The steering committee plays a critical role in making that strategic call and keeping campaign workers focused on the plan.

The organizational structure depicted in this chapter incorporates six teams within the citizens' campaign committee. Key responsibilities and activities of these six groups are summarized below.

COMMUNICATIONS

The communications committee's responsibility, preferably with the help and advice of a public relations professional with school tax campaign experience, is to translate the school district's information about the ballot proposal into a strong and persuasive advocacy campaign. *Translate* is used in this context to emphasize the importance of common messages—delivered in different styles and different media—coming from both the school district and citizens' committee. Achieving this requires close working relationships and common planning between key district staff and volunteers.

Key Communications Committee Responsibilities

Once the communications plan is ready, the committee supports the election effort by:

- Developing communications in alignment with core and subordinate themes and directed to target audiences.
- Developing brochures, press releases, letters, scripts, postcards, e-mails, and Web site presence as needed consistent with the campaign plan and schedule.
- Preparing and recruiting signers for letters to the editor consistent with campaign themes and the schedule of campaign activities.
- Mailing "yes" and "undecided" letters throughout canvassing.

One of the most common mistakes we encounter—often with unfortunate consequences—is turning volunteers loose without professional guidance or the prerequisite planning in place. It is absolutely critical that the research and planning phases be completed at the highest level *before* the communications committee's collective pen hits the paper in terms of producing pieces supporting the campaign. Establishing this foundational element well requires both expertise and time. Once this foundation is established, enforce a high level of message discipline as each individual communication is developed.

OUTREACH

As the name implies, the outreach committee focuses on key individuals and groups outside the school district's walls that will have a direct or indirect impact on the election's outcome. Although the focus is often on organized groups such as service clubs or business organizations, it is equally important to analyze the community's power structure to identify those individuals who need a courtesy call from someone from the campaign or school district. One way to generate such a list is to ask knowledgeable respondents to nominate at least five people in the community they believe will have the greatest impact on public opinion. After purging duplicates, the campaign will be left with a list of VIPs who need to be courted. We recommend that orchestrating these contacts be equally strategic through the use of ideal task performer and triangulation techniques from the campaign's toolkit. The effectiveness of these VIP encounters can be very different depending on who makes the contact and can often be more fruitful when two individuals (rather than one) interact with your targeted community opinion leaders.

Key Outreach Committee Responsibilities

The outreach committee focuses on efforts to connect with the community by:

- Identifying community influentials (individuals and groups).
- Setting up meetings and presentations with individuals and groups within the community with the intent of gaining support and minimizing opposition.
- Coordinating absentee voting for recent graduates.
- Planning and conducting coffee parties or other events focused on small group interactions.
- Coordinating voter registration and absentee ballot voting with parents using a fully annotated voter file and mapping.

In addition to working with individuals and groups within the community, the outreach committee is responsible for coordinating voter registration and absentee ballot voting with parents of school-age students and recent high school graduates (i.e., typically the last four graduation classes). With regard to voter registration efforts aimed at parents, demographic mapping techniques (presented in chapter 4) can be very helpful. Plotting parent households, registered voters, and voting history on your most recent election can provide the visual road map needed for targeted, door-to-door registration efforts in regions of the school district. The absentee ballot effort directed at recent graduates will be most effective if the campaign involves current high school students. The use of social networks like Facebook and MySpace as well as e-mail will facilitate ongoing contact with recent graduates.

The outreach committee's third responsibility is to plan appropriate and effective outreach activities designed to achieve small face-to-face group interactions. These initiatives are best symbolized by the coffee party paradigm. For many voters, a one-on-one conversation or small group encounter will ultimately make the difference. The goal should focus on creating dozens if not hundreds of face-to-face opportunities for the campaign to share its core message in a more personal and intimate forum. How this is done is left to the creativity of the committee based on the community's unique characteristics. A recent successful election in a Minnesota suburban district was buoyed by more than 100 coffee parties. Another campaign committee hosted numerous wine and cheese get-togethers. Speaking of captive audiences, a third school campaign delivered its message onboard a flotilla of pontoons on an area lake!

●

INREACH

The inreach committee contributes to the campaign effort by focusing efforts inside the walls of the district. First and foremost, the committee is soliciting support from employees. Building and maintaining such support throughout the campaign should never be taken for granted. Factors ranging from contract talks to employee grievances to where financial resources are targeted to go can and do impact attitudes among individuals and groups of employees. A common "war story" from the battles of unsuccessful school tax elections features the damaging effects of what employees said about the election after church or at the grocery store. While 100 percent support cannot be mandated nor guaranteed, you can build a foundation with good planning, information, and effective inreach to employees.

Key Inreach Committee Responsibilities

The inreach committee addresses the following important responsibilities and roles:

- Clarifying acceptable and unacceptable campaign activities by employees during the workday.
- Meeting with employees to provide information and answer questions.
- Working with union leaders of various employee groups.
- Soliciting financial support from employees and unions.
- Recruiting volunteers in support of campaign committees.

Wise campaign leaders will also revisit the school district's survey before finalizing plans related to involvement of key staff members or groups of employees. The optimal roles of the superintendent, principals, and teachers can best be determined when perceptions about these individuals and groups are tested in your local survey. It goes without saying that in some communities, the superintendent should be carrying the flag at the front of the parade. In your community, however, the role of the superintendent might best be played out behind closed doors or in a supporting role. The same can be said of teachers or other groups included in the polling results from your local taxpayers. If teachers are universally adored within the community, the campaign needs to craft a visible and prominent role for them in support of the election proposal.

When working inside the walls, use of ideal task performer strategies is equally effective as when stumping for support with the local Chamber of Commerce or Rotary Club. For example, a group of school district cooks will respond one way if the informational meeting is announced by the school district, and another way if the meeting is planned and announced jointly by one of their own leaders working in cooperation with the school district or citizens' campaign committee. If the leadership of the cooks' union is supportive of the election proposal, ask him or her to speak first at the informational meeting and then introduce district or campaign committee presenters. How campaign members approach and interact with employees can be just as important as the message and, as a result, significantly influence the meeting's effectiveness and outcome.

In addition to providing information and soliciting support, it is also important for the school district and staff working on the campaign to clarify for employees what they can and cannot do in support of the election, particularly during the workday. Although these parameters will vary from state to state, one could generalize that in many cases employees assume there are more restrictions on what they can say or do than actually is the case. It is often a political judgment rather than a legal question to determine the optimal level and nature of involvement of individual staff members and employee groups. Nevertheless, it is crucial for employees to understand the "do's and don'ts" early in the campaign, particularly as they relate to prohibitions in your state and the appropriate role for staff interacting with students at school.

CANVASSING

Voter canvassing is the campaign activity we most love to hate, and often the Achilles' heel of unsuccessful elections. When done comprehensively and strategically, canvassing provides the campaign with the essential ingredients for an effective get-out-the-vote (GOTV) strategy. Canvassing, in combination with post-election analysis, is also the best barometer as to whether the campaign is behind, on track, or well ahead of expectations. Although the intent of canvassing is commonly understood—to separate the universe of registered voters into "yes," "no," and "undecided"—it is methodology and use of data that separate the winners from the losers. The best approach recognizes the finite resources of time and money, takes full advantage of integrated databases, and concentrates efforts through the use of concentric canvassing targets.

Key Canvassing Committee Responsibilities

The canvassing committee focuses on these key activities:

- Conducting phone or door-to-door canvass using concentric target groups identified by the steering committee.
- Identifying "yes," "undecided," and "no" voters, and developing a systematic data storage and retrieval system to handle the results of the canvass.
- Soliciting names for endorsements and lawn signs.
- Providing names and addresses to the communications committee for mailings.
- Providing names, addresses, and phone numbers to the get-out-the-vote committee for GOTV efforts.

In most communities, the limitations of time, money, and volunteers inevitably limit the scope of canvassing, whether by foot or by phone. This reality should not, however, result in a random abstract approach using the local phone book or unidentified parcels on a demographic map. If your campaign either cannot or chooses not to canvass each and every household, it is incumbent that the campaign use available databases, survey results, count book, and mapping technology to canvass the *right* households in the *optimal* order. Again, finite campaign resources need to be targeted to maximize return in terms of identifying support and eventually getting it to the polls on election day. Canvassing done in this manner—whether it is door to door or by telephone—uses a fully annotated voter file in which a set of concentric target groups has been defined.

Identification of targeted groups within the context of registered voters is nothing new to partisan elections, but it has been little used in school district campaigns. Setting concentric targets for canvassing begins by asking three key questions:

- Where is your support? Answer: Look at your survey.
- How many individuals belong to that particular voting bloc? Answer: Look at your count book.
- How likely is it that this bloc of individuals will vote? Answer: Look at your voter history.

Through strategic use of these complementary planning resources, the campaign's steering committee can establish concentric targets similar to the following example:

- Target 1: Registered parents who are also frequent voters.
- Target 2: Registered parents who are infrequent voters.
- Target 3: Alumni parents (youngest child has graduated from public schools).
- Target 4: Parents of preschoolers (oldest child has not yet entered public school).
- Target 5: Voters who have made donations to your public school foundation.
- Target 6: Past supporters.
- Target 7: Democrats (if your database identifies party and survey results indicate Democrats are more supportive).
- Target 8: Registered voters who always vote in school district elections.

While the makeup of the concentric target groups will vary from district to district, the strategy remains the same—start at the core with the largest bloc of supportive voters (based on survey results and count book), and who also have the best voting records (based on post-election analysis). From the inside out—moving through one target group after another—the canvassing process identifies supporters, and in so doing, it inches ever closer to the target number of "yes" voters needed on election day. Being thoughtful and strategic about *whom* you talk to and *when* also benefits the election campaign by avoiding wasting time on the wrong voters. A door-to-door canvass can benefit from the same strategy and obtain similarly positive results using a fully annotated voter file and mapping technology. Skillful use of these resources will send door-to-door canvassers to the right homes using the identical concentric targeting approach.

Canvassing on a platform of a fully annotated voter file also pays dividends late in the campaign. Let's say it is November 2 and the campaign has one day left before election day and there are 800 voters on the "undecided" list based on canvassing. Assuming the campaign is still 300 votes short of its target in terms of needed "yes" votes, there is a need to dust off and revisit this "undecided" pool of potential voters. With only hours to go before the polls open, how might the citizens' committee approach this challenge? The best approach might be to identify and pull a second set of concentric targets focused only on the 800 "undecided" voters. Target 1 could be "undecided" parents among that group who have been frequent voters in the past. Once the parent bloc is exhausted, the campaign could turn its attention to alumni parents who are frequent voters. The third target from this group of "undecided" voters might be younger adults with preschool children. Again, the point is that time and human resources are finite commodities—being strategic and setting priorities related to which voters among the 800 "undecided" to interact with can be the difference between winning and losing the election. Use of a fully annotated voter file and concentric strategies allows the campaign to produce targeted lists instantaneously and is far more effective than simply working through an alphabetical list.

This general approach also applies after the canvassing is done as the steering committee determines how to use the canvassing data to its best advantage from the conclusion of canvassing through election day. Figure 11.2 shows a chart produced by Todd Rapp of Himle Horner, Inc., and reflects this parallel strategy by depicting the concentration of campaign

	Supporter	**Undecided**	**Opponent**
Very Likely Voter	GOTV	Heavy Persuasion	Neutralize
Somewhat Likely Voter	Persuasion & GOTV	Moderate Persuasion	Ignore
Unlikely Voter	Persuasion	Supporter	Ignore

Figure 11.2. Targeting Voters

resources in direct relationship to the disposition and voting records of residents within the school district. As reflected in this graphic, how the citizens' committee engages with different blocs of voters should vary depending on the level of support and the likelihood of individuals and groups to cast ballots.

Based on successful practices in many school tax elections, we are also able to recommend the following tactical approaches that, in combination, can mean the difference between a successful and disappointing canvass:

- Use multiple canvassing teams, each working two or three nights, rather than one team of canvassers taking on the entire project. This approach makes it easier to recruit volunteers (e.g., "You only have to work two nights"). It also avoids burnout, and it significantly expands the number of individuals involved in the campaign.
- Set your campaign target at 130 percent of your best-educated guess in terms of the number of "yes" voters you need to deliver to the polls on election day. This strategy provides the campaign with a margin and allows for some slippage for misidentified "yes" voters or a less-than-stellar GOTV effort on election day.
- Discount identified male supporters by 0.25 to reflect three realities about male voters: compared with women voters, they are less likely to vote in a school election, more likely to be Republican than Democrat, and less likely to be supportive of a school finance proposal (Flanigan and Zingale, 1998). If a two-voter household (one male and one female) were canvassed using this tactic, and two "yes" votes were identified, the household would be counted as 1.75 "yes" votes on the way to the campaign target. Again, this approach provides some margin and, in combination with the 130 percent tactic, avoids the mistake of overestimating support.
- Conduct phone canvassing at a central location, after volunteers have been trained, and with the support of at least one, and preferably two, representatives from the school administration or school board in attendance.
- When phone canvassing, always have two more lines (whether land lines or cell phones) available than volunteer callers. This allows volunteers to hand off more difficult calls to an administrator or school board member without having to wait for that line to clear before continuing

the canvassing. Begin making contact with voters after they have received information in the mail concerning the district's proposal. Cold calling is difficult and produces far too many undecided voters.

- Plan ahead for the handling of data and record-keeping before the canvassing process begins. This can range from paper and pencil (not recommended) to managing your own databases to using sophisticated campaign software specifically designed for school elections. Regardless of your approach, you need to record accurately and be able to effectively use the data for communications and GOTV efforts.

FINANCE

The finance committee's role is fairly straightforward, with only one significant recommendation based on best practices across the country. Similar to our earlier emphasis that districts should never start writing a proposal before the research and planning steps are done, finance committees are wise to delay fundraising until the school board is clear on the ballot question and the steering committee has determined how much money is needed and for what purpose. Raising money is seldom easy, but it is certainly more daunting when those asking for the money do not know for certain what the election is about and how the citizens' committee intends to use requested donations. In all cases, the finance committee needs to check on all applicable campaign finance laws and regulations. The finance chair and campaign treasurer must ensure that all required campaign finance reports are filed accurately and on time.

Key Finance Committee Responsibilities

The key activities of the finance committee are:

- Soliciting sufficient donations to finance the campaign activities developed by the steering committee.
- Monitoring committee budgets.
- Maintaining records of receipts and expenses.
- Completing required financial reports during and after the election.

It is the steering committee's responsibility to determine what is needed to win the election (e.g., election consultation, scientific survey, demographic mapping, public relations expertise, or database management) and the funding needed to pay for these resources. Once the school board has finalized the ballot proposal and the steering committee has approved a campaign budget, the finance committee has its walking orders. Strategies for raising the needed resources will vary from community to community, but one variable is constant: if the committee cannot raise the necessary money to run a winning campaign, it probably cannot win the election.

GET-OUT-THE-VOTE EFFORTS

It is not often possible for a school district to know exactly how it won an election, but occasionally it happens, and in most cases, it involves the efforts of the get-out-the-vote committee. A district on the peninsula south of San Francisco was lucky enough to learn they won thanks to one of the last phone calls they made on election day. That evening, as the votes were being counted, they failed to win the two-thirds majority required for passage in California. Their only hope was the provisional ballots, which the county would count the following Thursday. They gathered at the election office on Thursday afternoon to watch the final vote count and, to their great relief, ended up winning the supermajority they needed by one vote. Before he left, one of the election workers tapped the superintendent on the shoulder and said he knew exactly how they got that one vote. He had been a poll worker on election day, and as he was preparing to close the polling place, he spotted a woman running at full speed down the street. With hair and jacket flying in all directions and out of breath, she reached the polls just before they were to close. The poll worker told her to catch her breath. She was going to be able to vote. When she had composed herself, she thanked him and told him she had forgotten about the election but had just received a call from a friend working on the campaign reminding her that the polls were still open. That call produced the one-vote margin the district needed. In all their subsequent elections, they knew just how valuable GOTV efforts are to a successful effort.

By permission of John L. Hart FLP and Creators Syndicate, Inc.

The activity of the GOTV committee is short-lived but critical to the success of a school operating or facility referendum. Unfortunately, many school tax elections are planned and executed at a very high level only to falter on election day with a woefully inadequate GOTV effort. How do research and best practice inform school leaders in terms of achieving better success in getting supporters to cast ballots? The northern California district mentioned above was obviously on the right track.

Donald P. Green and Alan S. Gerber are Yale University political scientists, GOTV researchers, and authors of *Get Out the Vote! How to Increase Voter Turnout*, which was published by the Brookings Institution. They have teamed up on dozens of controlled experiments testing the effectiveness of different types of GOTV strategies. Their experiments have been conducted in municipal, state, and issues-based contests in rural, suburban, and urban environments across the country. Their research focuses on one key question: *What are the most cost-effective ways to increase voter turnout?*

Green and Gerber employ research designs in which voters are randomly assigned to experimental and control groups and then subjected to different types of GOTV strategies. Much of their research points to a direct correlation between face-to-face efforts and substantially better turnouts at the polls. Whether it's hip-hop or an old-fashioned midwestern potluck, these researchers challenge school leaders to meaningfully engage supporters on a personal level to improve GOTV success on election day.

Although most of their research has not focused specifically on school elections, Green recounts one experiment conducted during a 2001 school board race in Bridgeport, Connecticut. Although the 9.9 percent turnout was abysmal, turnout among voters who were canvassed face-to-face by

a campaign worker increased 14 percent compared with those who were
not canvassed. "That's another sign of the importance of establishing a
personal connection between voters and the electoral process," explains
Green.

The five GOTV strategies that Green and Gerber investigated should
be familiar to school leaders experienced in planning construction and
operating campaigns. These strategies are:

- Face-to-face canvassing.
- Leafleting (specifically door hangers in this context).
- Direct mail.
- Telephone calls.
- E-mail.

The authors have quantified the number of additional votes one can expect
based on how many contacts were made using each of the five strategies.
These data also allow the campaign to estimate the approximate cost per
additional vote if the campaign hires canvassers instead of using volunteers. The results of their research—in terms of how commonly used
GOTV initiatives affect turnout—*might* surprise you:

- Door-to-door canvassing resulted in one additional vote per 14 con-
  tacts.
- Reminder calling resulted in one additional vote per 66 contacts.
- Direct mail resulted in one additional vote per 177 contacts.
- E-mail had no detectable effect.

It's important to note that the researchers consider the positive effect
of door-to-door canvassing (one vote per 14 contacts) as a conservative
estimate of its value. Related GOTV research also documents the secondary benefit of face-to-face canvassing in terms of higher voting patterns
by individuals in the same household. Although not canvassed directly,
voting patterns by other household members also increase, apparently as
a result of interactions with the individual who was actually canvassed.
In summarizing their research, Green and Gerber emphasized two key
conclusions:

- To mobilize voters, you must make them feel wanted at the polls. Mobilizing voters is rather like inviting them to a social occasion. Personal invitations convey the most warmth and effort.
- Building on voters' pre-existing levels of motivation to vote is also important. Frequent voters, by definition, have demonstrated their willingness to participate in the electoral process. In low-turnout elections, they are especially receptive to GOTV appeals, particularly when contacted face to face.

Green and Gerber also introduce the notion of *supertreatments* to improve a campaign's GOTV success. In this context, supertreatment refers to the kinds of contacts that are likely to be especially effective, such as contacts from close friends, coworkers, or the candidate in a partisan election. For example, the researchers suggest that anonymous e-mail appears to do little to increase voter turnout as compared to e-mail from friends, neighbors, or business associates.

Effectively applying GOTV research also requires that the campaign reject the one-size-fits-all approach and target different GOTV strategies on unique blocs of voters. Individuals within your community have marked different predispositions to vote. Using the most effective GOTV strategies will not optimize turnout if all voters are treated similarly. Consider the differences among the following three voters, all of whom were identified as supporters in a recent pre-election canvass:

- Voter 1 is a 42-year-old female who is a parent of a public school student, was active on the school board campaign committee, and has voted in 100 percent of the past five elections within the jurisdiction.
- Voter 2 is a 28-year-old single male who has voted in 20 percent of the past five elections within the jurisdiction.
- Voter 3 is a 68-year-old female who has voted in 60 percent of the past five elections within the jurisdiction.

Each of these voters has been identified by the campaign as supportive of the district tax proposal. How should the campaign approach GOTV with these three voters?

For Voter 1, we would suggest that anything more than a reminder call on election day is a waste of the campaign's time and resources. She is going to vote and she is going to vote "yes." Voter 2 is quite another animal, so to speak. In addition to any literature drops, mailings, and reminder calls, this voter needs a personal contact on election day, preferably from someone he knows or a peer. Voter 2 would also have been a good candidate for an absentee ballot voting initiative. Urging Voter 2 to apply for an absentee ballot significantly lengthens election day, giving the campaign more opportunities to remind him to actually cast his "yes" vote. It will take an extraordinary effort to get him to the polls.

In *Politics the Wellstone Way* (Wellstone Action, 2005), the authors reinforce the need to respond differently to this type of voter, challenging campaigns to develop up to seven different GOTV interventions for the most reticent voters. One simple example will illustrate. A school district with a very solid record of success at the polls always identifies all of the supporters who fit into the Less Active or New Voter category and makes them the target of a multicontact "Dear Friend" postcard effort. This addition to all of the other GOTV efforts they apply to all identified support always increases turnout in this group of voters. The count book (chapter 2) and the post-election analysis (chapter 3) provide the campaign with the data to differentiate its GOTV strategies based on demographics and past participation in similar elections.

Voter 3 is "on the bubble" and will require more than a call or door hanger. A phone call from a friend or at least a peer or the offer of a ride from a friend will dramatically improve the odds of delivering her "yes" vote on election day.

The most perplexing group for many school tax elections is young adults. Notwithstanding the recent success of the Obama campaign, engaging 18- to 34-year-old voters and getting them to the polls on election day constitute a major challenge, one that extends to school tax elections. Ironically, while 80 percent of young voters typically fail to vote, survey research often finds that the strongest support for school district proposals comes from this demographic group. The Pew Charitable Trusts (Skaggs and Anthony, 2003), for example, reports that education was at the top of the list of important issues based on a national survey of 1,500 young adults conducted in 2002. *If* you can get them to the polls, this group will largely vote "yes."

Poor turnout by young voters—both parents and nonparents—has been evident in school tax elections from New Jersey to California. Post-election analyses from recent Minnesota elections conducted by the Center for Community Opinion and Political Design documented turnouts by 18- to 34-year-old voters averaging about 18 percent. Parents in this age range did not perform much better, with around 25 percent typically casting a ballot.

It is a daunting challenge for the GOTV team when the strongest support for the school district's proposal resides in the demographic group least likely to show up. Effectively engaging and delivering young adults to the voting booth on election day requires that the campaign leadership understand and implement GOTV strategies based on solid research and successful practice.

Green and Gerber's research also concludes that GOTV interventions are more effective the closer they are to election day. At a minimum, this suggests that GOTV calls be done on election day (unless prohibited by state law) or as close to election day as possible. Successful practice and common sense dictate the reminder calls be *on election day* rather than a day or two before for the same reason that one would set a Palm Pilot alarm on your wedding anniversary if the purpose were to pick up flowers on the way home. Having the alarm ring (GOTV reminder call) on Monday to remember to pick up flowers (vote) on Tuesday does not have the same sense of urgency. A message of "The polls are open now and we anticipate a very close vote" is more likely to get a voter off the couch and to the polls as opposed to "Don't forget to vote tomorrow." If your campaign wants to build repetitive contact into the last weekend of the campaign because you can see in the voter file that much of your support has a weak voting history, call supporters on Sunday afternoon to let them know where their polling place will be located. Then follow with a GOTV call on election day.[2]

Key Get-Out-the-Vote Committee Responsibilities

The key activities of the GOTV committee are:

- Delivering every identified "yes" voter to the ballot box through either absentee voting or participation on election day.

- Completing reminder calls, e-mail contacts, and targeted door-to-door efforts on election day.
- Providing transportation to any "yes" voter needing a ride to the polls.
- Providing childcare to any "yes" voter needing such assistance to vote.

Depending on your state's election laws, GOTV efforts sometimes include poll watching or, in states with same-day registration, election day efforts to get supporters registered to vote. These activities vary greatly due to restrictions in poll-watching tactics and same-day registration at the polls in many states. The advent of all-mail ballot elections and the ability of voters in some states to register as permanent absentee voters will also impact the way in which your campaign approaches GOTV.

Plotting parent and voter history data on demographic maps also provides resources that can be used by the GOTV committee either on election day (if not prohibited by law) or in the days leading up to election day. Although most campaign committees use the telephone for GOTV efforts, demographic maps can help campaigners pinpoint specific areas, streets, or neighborhoods that warrant a targeted door-to-door effort to supplement reminder calls. Demographic mapping, for example, might identify 10 adjacent homes on a particular street, all of which contain public school students with parents who are either unregistered or have very infrequent voting habits. The mapping provides the needed information to surgically deploy a team of volunteers to a specific grouping of homes to improve GOTV results. In our experience, we have seen school tax campaigns pull anywhere from 33 percent to 95 percent of its supporters to the polls depending on the effectiveness of the campaign and the GOTV committee's execution.

DEALING WITH ORGANIZED OPPOSITION

Many factors will influence if and when organized opposition might emerge in your campaign.[3] If it does, you need to be prepared to deal with the distraction it will produce. The word *distraction* is used with great purpose here because the first thing opposition produces is distraction. All of the energy your campaign committee has poured into its efforts to promote and communicate could be rechanneled overnight into phone calls, e-mail exchanges, and emergency meetings intended to counter opposition. As a result, your opponents have the ability to waste many valuable volunteer hours.

To blunt this effect, some campaigns have organized a "rear guard" to deal with the distraction opponents can generate. The members of this part of the campaign team are responsible for handling anything done by the opposition while the rest of the campaign continues to execute the plan it developed to inform, identify, and reinforce "yes" votes. By absorbing the impact the opposition is attempting to have on the entire campaign, the rear guard helps keep the overall campaign on track and on target.

While the nature of the opponents that emerge in your district will shape the message they will present to the community, this will not be an effort to communicate as much as an attempt to disrupt your communication efforts and confuse the voters. Remember that your opponent's primary goal is to defeat your tax proposal, not engage in a debate.

While you must deliver clear, concise information to the voters to generate "yes" votes, an opposition group only needs to create confusion and doubt to create "no" votes. As a result, you need to ensure the campaign maintains its focus and does not let opposition take it off plan or off message. It is essential that the bulk of the campaign's energy keeps moving toward victory on election day.

If organized opposition emerges during your campaign, there are some specific rules we suggest you follow. First, make sure your campaign sticks to its campaign and communications plan. You may need to modify that plan to deal with the elements the opposition has introduced. But if you abandon your campaign plan entirely, you have, in essence, turned the leadership of your effort over to the opposition.

Second, respond to items the opposition introduces in a way that keeps your primary message in front of the voters. This can be accomplished by following the 80/20 rule: 80 percent of your response should present your primary argument for the tax proposal while only 20 percent of your response should be used to address the opposition's arguments. In doing so, however, you should ensure you do not overrespond. For example, instead of assuming you need to use every medium available to you, the campaign should respond only in the medium selected by the opponents. You want to avoid situations where your campaign introduces the arguments of your opponents to voters who might otherwise never come across those ideas.

Third, do not be afraid to dismiss the opposition as individuals who are opposed to all tax proposals or to the basic idea that we should have good public schools in the United States. Never assume the voters of your district know that what at first appears to be new ideas introduced by the opposition might in fact be long-standing antitax or antigovernment arguments that can be found in abundance on the Internet. You also may need to tell your voters not to be confused by the misinformation introduced by organized opposition.

Fourth, remember your best weapon is the "light" created by clear, concise information about the district's needs and its tax proposal. Opposition groups do their best work in the shadows where their innuendos and assertions can fester unchallenged. Do not be afraid to draw the opposition into the bright light of the public forum. This does not mean you immediately challenge them to a debate. Rather, it does mean you take sufficient information about them, their background, and your proposal to the press and to community leaders. You also make sure all of your volunteers and district staff are well briefed and prepared to confidently rebut any of the opponent's statements should they hear them repeated among their friends and neighbors.

Finally, remember that all of your actions are part of a political campaign. Success on election day is the goal, and every action you take must be planned and executed to move your proposal one step closer to that goal. As an educator, you may feel a strong impulse to educate and explain, but you may have to rein in that impulse. Instead, measure and plan your responses to blunt the impact of your opponents and achieve your original goal—stronger classroom programs or better school facilities for students.

If we were to summarize this chapter in just two words, it would be "campaigning matters!" It is incumbent upon the superintendent and campaign leadership to first understand and avail themselves of both research and best practice. Once the campaign plan is developed, it is vital that it be executed in world-class fashion—coordinated between the school district and citizens' campaign committee—based not only on research and successful practice, but also on the unique culture of your school community. The margins between winning and losing are just too slim to do anything less.

NOTES

1. Check to make sure there are not laws in your state that attempt to limit the role of school board members.

2. In campaigns that combine a Sunday night call about the polling place location and a GOTV call on election day, volunteers and campaign leaders are always astonished at the number of people who forgot about the election on election day despite a call two nights earlier.

3. This material on organized opposition was included in "Managing Organized Opposition," published in *School Administrator*, American Association of School Administrators, April 2008.

A Final Thought

We find ourselves rewriting this book at a very stressful time for public school districts across the country. In spring 2009, there were some estimates that as many as 575,000 teachers would be laid off before the start of the new school year in September. Even dealing with the limited number of districts we serve as clients, we have sat through extremely difficult and emotional school board meetings where parents and students expressed their concerns as talented teachers were told their jobs might not exist next fall. Many of these meetings are like the film Mr. Holland's Opus come to life.

It is our hope that by expanding our election research, strategies, and tactics, school leaders in all parts of the country might find ways to successfully reach out to their own communities. We know there is no magic bullet buried in the pages of prose that make up this book. It is our sincere hope, however, that by sharing all we have learned over more than 20 years of work with superintendents, board members, and parents, friends of education everywhere will find in our ideas ways to harness the energy and ideals of their own communities and take the steps needed to protect all that public education has to offer this generation and the next.

Bibliography

Allen, A. L. (1985). Predictors of voting behavior in school financial referenda (doctoral dissertation, University of Missouri, Columbia, 1985). *Dissertation Abstracts International*, 47, 719.

Beckham, J. D. (2001). An examination of the influence of technology inclusion in determining the outcome of school bond issue elections in Oklahoma (doctoral dissertation, University of Oklahoma, 2001). *Dissertation Abstracts International*, 62, 85.

Blount, K. D. (1991). The relationship between school tax election outcomes, selected population characteristics, and selected campaign strategies in Louisiana from 1985–1990 (doctoral dissertation, University of Southern Mississippi, 1991). *Dissertation Abstracts International*, 52, 3180.

Bolman, L. G., & Deal, T. E. (1991). *Reframing organization: Artistry, choice, and leadership*. San Francisco, Calif.: Jossey-Bass.

Brummer, K. C. (1999). School bond elections in Iowa: An analysis of factors, strategies, and policies that influence outcomes (doctoral dissertation, Drake University, 1999). *Dissertation Abstracts International*, 61, 2538.

Chandler, J. A. (1989). A comparison of the predictability rates of the Lutz dissatisfaction and school bond election models of local school district politics in selected Oklahoma school districts, 1971–1989 (doctoral dissertation, University of Tulsa, 1989). *Dissertation Abstracts International*, 52, 30.

Clemens, A. D. (2003). Issues and related strategies used in successful school facilities bond elections in seven selected Orange county school districts between June 2000 to March 2002 (doctoral dissertation, University of La Verne, 2003). ProQuest Dissertations and Theses, Section 0476, Part 0514.

Corrick, C. C. (1995). Voter perceptions, information, and demographic characteristics as critical factors in successful and unsuccessful bond referenda in selected Kansas school districts: 1988–1990 (doctoral dissertation, Kansas State University, 1995). *Dissertation Abstracts International*, 56, 2054.

Dalton, R. A. (1995). Local general obligation bonds: Factors which have influenced the outcome of school district elections (doctoral dissertation, University of Southern California, 1995). *Dissertation Abstracts International*, 57, 44.

Day, D. V. (1996). Influences on a community college bond election: A case study (doctoral dissertation, University of Kansas, 1996). *Dissertation Abstracts International*, 57, 2336.

Dunbar, D. W. (1991). A comparison of mail ballot elections and polling place elections for school bond issues in Kansas (elections) (doctoral dissertation, Oklahoma State University, 1991). *Dissertation Abstracts International*, 52, 3180.

Etheredge, F. D. (1989). *School boards and the ballot box*. Alexandria, Va.: National School Boards Association.

Faltys, D. J. (2006). Factors influencing the successful passage of a school bond referendum as identified by selected voters in the Navasota Independent School District in Texas (doctoral dissertation, Texas A&M University, 2006). ProQuest Dissertations and Theses, Section 0803, Part 0277.

Flanigan, W. H., & Zingale, N. H. (1998). *Political behavior and the American electorate* (9th ed.). Washington, D.C.: CQ Press.

Franklin, G. A. (1997). School finance campaigns: Strategies and other factors related to success (voters) (doctoral dissertation, University of Southern California, 1997). *Dissertation Abstracts International*, 58, 1595.

Friedland, H. A. (2002). The ecology of school bond elections: Factors associated with election results in New Jersey (doctoral dissertation, Columbia University Teachers College, 2002). ProQuest Dissertations and Theses, Section 0055, Part 0514.

Galton, L. L. (1996). Understanding the reasons for and impact of one small Massachusetts community's lack of fiscal support for its local school system, 1990–1993 (doctoral dissertation, Harvard University, 1996). *Dissertation Abstracts International*, 57, 944.

Geurink, G. (2008). An analysis of factors leading to the passage of school district finance referenda within the State of Wisconsin (doctoral dissertation, Edgewood College, 2008). ProQuest Dissertations and Theses, Section 0501, Part 0277.

Grady-Hahn, L. F. (1999) School levy failures: A look at causes and cures (master's dissertation, Pacific Lutheran University, 1999). ProQuest Dissertations and Theses, Section 6200, Part 0514.

Hallene, A. F., Jr. (1999). Development of a logistic regression methodology for predicting K–12 education tax rate increase referenda outcomes by individual school district (doctoral dissertation, University of Iowa, 1999). ProQuest Dissertations and Theses, Section 0096, Part 0546.

Henderson, J. F., Jr. (1986). Revenue election campaign strategies used in Colorado school districts which conducted successful and unsuccessful elections for 1981–1985 (doctoral dissertation, University of Colorado, Boulder, 1986). *Dissertation Abstracts International*, 58, 2542.

Hickey, W. D. (2004). A survey of superintendent emotional intelligence as a factor in bond election outcomes (doctoral dissertation, Austin State University, 2004). ProQuest Dissertations and Theses, Section 6340, Part 0514.

Hinson, J. L. (2001). A study of the relationship between the outcome of school district bond issue elections and selected variables (doctoral dissertation, Saint Louis University, 2001). *Dissertation Abstracts International*, 62, 1652.

Hockersmith, D. C. (2001). Strategies used by school district superintendents, chief business officials, and school board members to achieve acquisition of a general obligation bond (doctoral dissertation, University of La Verne, 2001). *Dissertation Abstracts International*, 61, 4627.

Kimbrough, R. B., & Nunnery, M. Y. (1971). *Politics, power, polls, and school elections*. Berkeley, Calif.: McCutchan.

Kinsall, M. L. (2000). A study of the effects of election campaign strategies on successful passage of tax levies (doctoral dissertation, Saint Louis University, 2000). ProQuest Dissertations and Theses, Section 0193, Part 0277.

Lake, C. C., & Callbeck Harper, P. (1987). *Public opinion polling: A handbook for public interest and citizen advocacy groups*. Washington, D.C.: Island.

Lifto, D. E. (2005, March–April). School finance elections: Hip-hop to victory. *Minnesota School Boards Association Journal*.

———. (2001, November). Lessons from the bond battlefield. *American School Board Journal*.

Lifto, D. E., & Morris, W. (2001, March–April). Q4C referendums. *Minnesota School Boards Association Journal*.

———. (2000). Drivers of successful bond and operating levies . . . Q4C at the foundation. *School Business Affairs*, 66(10), 15–17.

Lifto, D. E., & Parsons, R. W. (1998, November). So you've lost the bond or referendum election—what do you do now? *School Business Affairs*.

Lifto, D. E., and Senden, J. B. (2009, May). Transforming white light into rainbows: segmentation strategies for successful school tax elections. *School Business Affairs*.

———. (2009, March–April). Understanding alumni parents and school voting tendencies. *Minnesota School Boards Association Journal*.

———. (2008, April). Managing organized opposition. *School Administrator*.

———. (2006, February). Watch your language: Words to win by in your next school finance campaign. *School Administrator*.

———. (2005, April). The case of precinct 5. *American School Board Journal*.

———. (2004). *School finance elections: A comprehensive planning model for success*. Scarecrow Press and the American Association of School Administrators.

——. (2004, January). Examining elections past. *School Administrator.*

——. (2003, February). Finding success at the ballot box. *Managing School Business.*

——. (2002, November). Concentric canvassing: Finding success from the inside out. *School Business Affairs.*

——. (2002, February–March). Budget battles at the ballot box. *Minnesota School Boards Association Journal.*

Lode, M. D. (1999). Factors affecting the outcomes of school bond elections in Iowa (doctoral dissertation, University of South Dakota, 1999). *Dissertation Abstracts International*, 60, 2310.

National School Public Relations Association. (2002). *Raising the bar for school PR: New standards for the school public relations profession.* Rockville, Md.: Author.

Neill, S. W. (2003). The identification of effective strategies for bond campaigns in Kansas school districts: An analysis of the beliefs of superintendents who conducted bond issue campaigns (doctoral dissertation, Wichita State University, 2003). ProQuest Dissertations and Theses, Section 0260, Part 0514.

Pappalardo, J. W., Jr. (2005). Strategies used by superintendents, chief business officials, and school board members in successful Proposition 39 general education bond elections (doctoral dissertation, University of La Verne, 2005). ProQuest Dissertations and Theses, Section 0476, Part 0277.

Phillips, C. T. (1995). An investigation of strategies related to successful and unsuccessful campaigns for passage of school operating issues in Ohio (doctoral dissertation, University of Akron, 1995). *Dissertation Abstracts International*, 56, 1610.

Piele, P., & Hall, J. (1973). *Budgets, bonds, and ballots.* Lexington, Mass.: Heath.

Pullium, T. N. (1983). A study of selected factors associated with the success and failure of school bond referenda in the state of Georgia during the decade of the 1970s (doctoral dissertation, University of Georgia, 1983). *Dissertation Abstracts International*, 44, 1281).

Sclafani, S. (1985). The determinants of school budget election outcomes in New York State: A forecasting model (doctoral dissertation, Rutgers State University, 1985). *Dissertation Abstracts International*, 47, 83.

Stockton, D. J. (1996). Influences contributing to the successful passage of a school bond referendum in the Conroe Independent School District (Texas, tax levy) (doctoral dissertation, Texas A&M University, 1996). *Dissertation Abstracts International*, 57, 2312.

True, N. B. (1996). Factors affecting the passage or defeat of California school districts' parcel tax measures between 1983 and 1994 (doctoral dissertation, University of San Francisco, 1996). *Dissertation Abstracts International*, 57, 1496.

Wellstone Action. (2005). *Politics the Wellstone way*. Minneapolis: University of Minnesota Press.

Williamson, S. G. (1997). Factors influencing voter behavior in school board elections (doctoral dissertation, Texas A&M University, Commerce, 1997). *Dissertation Abstracts International*, 58, 3015.

About the Authors

Don E. Lifto, Ph.D., is senior vice president and director of the Public Education Group at Springsted Incorporated, a public finance advisory and consulting firm based in St. Paul, Minnesota. He previously served as a public school superintendent in Minnesota for 25 years. Lifto's Ph.D. dissertation focused on strategic factors, nonstrategic factors, and critical incidents affecting the outcome of school finance elections. He writes, presents, and consults on this topic frequently.

J. Bradford Senden, Ph.D., has helped school districts throughout the country to plan and execute successful school tax campaigns for the past 20 years. He is managing partner of the Center for Community Opinion, which specializes in survey research and data preparation needed to win tax elections. He writes, presents, and consults on this topic frequently.